DEAD SILENCE

The Legacy of Human Rights Abuses in Punjab

Human Rights Watch/Asia
(formerly Asia Watch)

Physicians for Human Rights

Human Rights Watch
New York • Washington • Los Angeles • London

Copyright © May 1994 by Human Rights Watch and Physicians for Human Rights
All rights reserved.
Printed in the United States of America.

ISBN 1-56432-130-4
LCCCN: 94-75428

Human Rights Watch/Asia (formerly Asia Watch)
Human Rights Watch/Asia was established in 1985 to monitor and promote the observance of internationally recognized human rights in Asia. Sidney Jones is the executive director; Mike Jendrzejczyk is the Washington director; Robin Munro is the Hong Kong director; Therese Caouette, Patricia Gossman and Jeannine Guthrie are research associates; Cathy Yai-Wen Lee and Grace Oboma-Layat are associates; Mickey Spiegel is a research consultant. Jack Greenberg is the chair of the advisory committee and Orville Schell is vice chair.

Physicians for Human Rights
Physicians for Human Rights (PHR) is an organization of physicians and other health professionals that brings the knowledge and skills of the medical sciences to the investigation and prevention of violations of international human rights and humanitarian law. PHR works to apply the special skills of health professionals to stop torture, "disappearances" and political killings by governments and opposition groups; to report on conditions and protection of detainees in prisons and refugee camps; to investigate the physical and psychological consequences of violations of humanitarian law and medical ethics in internal and international conflicts; to defend the right of civilians and combatants to receive medical care during times of war; to protect health professionals who are victims of human rights abuses; and to prevent medical complicity in torture and other human rights abuses.
Since 1986, PHR has sent over 40 fact-finding and emergency missions to over 25 countries. PHR bases its actions on the Universal Declaration of Human Rights and other international human rights and humanitarian agreements. The organization adheres to a policy of strict impartiality and is concerned with the medical consequences of human rights abuses regardless of the ideology of the offending government or group.
H. Jack Geiger, M.D. is President; Carola Eisenberg, M.D. is Vice President. The Board of Directors includes: Holly G. Atkinson, M.D.; Hon. J. Kenneth Blackwell; Kevin Cahill, M.D.; Charles Clements, M.D.; John Constable, M.D.; Robert Cook-Deegan, M.D.; Paul Epstein, M.D. ; Robert Kirchner, M.D.; Jennifer Learning, M.D.; Aryeh Neier; Jane Green Schaller, M.D.; M. Roy Schwarz, M.D.; Kim Thorburn, M.D.; Philippe Villers, M.D.
The staff includes: Eric Stover, executive director; Susannah Sirkin, deputy director; Kari Hannibal, membership and education coordinator; Gina VanderLoop, development director; Barbara Ayotte, senior program associate; Shana Swiss, M.D., director of Women's Program; Vincent Iacopino, M.D., Western Regional Representative; and Clyde C. Snow, senior forensic consultant.
The address for Physicians for Human Rights is 100 Boylston Street, Suite 702, Boston, MA 02116, Tel: (617) 695-0041, Fax: (617) 695-0307, email: phrusa@igc.apc.org

HUMAN RIGHTS WATCH

Human Rights Watch conducts regular, systematic investigations of human rights abuses in some seventy countries around the world. It addresses the human rights practices of governments of all political stripes, of all geopolitical alignments, and of all ethnic and religious persuasions. In internal wars it documents violations by both governments and rebel groups. Human Rights Watch defends freedom of thought and expression, due process and equal protection of the law; it documents and denounces murders, disappearances, torture, arbitrary imprisonment, exile, censorship and other abuses of internationally recognized human rights.

Human Rights Watch began in 1978 with the founding of its Helsinki division. Today, it includes five divisions covering Africa, the Americas, Asia, the Middle East, as well as the signatories of the Helsinki accords. It also includes five collaborative projects on arms, children's rights, free expression, prison conditions, and women's rights. It maintains offices in New York, Washington, Los Angeles, London, Brussels, Moscow, Belgrade, Zagreb and Hong Kong. Human Rights Watch is an independent, nongovernmental organization, supported by contributions from private individuals and foundations. It accepts no government funds, directly or indirectly.

The staff includes Kenneth Roth, executive director; Cynthia Brown, program director; Holly J. Burkhalter, advocacy director; Allyson Collins, research associate; Richard Dicker, associate counsel; Jamie Fellner, foundation relations director; Hamilton Fish, Jr., senior advisor; Barbara Guglielmo, controller; Robert Kimzey, publications director; Gara LaMarche, associate director; Liselotte Leicht, Brussels office director; Michal Longfelder, development director; Ellen Lutz, California director; Juan Méndez, general counsel; Susan Osnos, communications director; Jemera Rone, counsel; Rachel Weintraub, special events director; and Derrick Wong, finance and administration director.

The regional directors of Human Rights Watch are Abdullahi An-Na'im, Africa; Cindy Arnson and Anne Manuel (acting directors), Americas; Sidney Jones, Asia; Jeri Laber, Helsinki; and Christopher George, Middle East. The project directors are Kenneth Anderson, Arms Project; Lois Whitman, Children's Rights Project; Gara LaMarche, Free Expression Project; Joanna Weschler, Prison Project; and Dorothy Q. Thomas, Women's Rights Project.

The board includes Robert L. Bernstein, chair; Adrian W. DeWind, vice chair; Roland Algrant, Lisa Anderson, Peter D. Bell, Alice L. Brown, William Carmichael, Dorothy Cullman, Irene Diamond, Jonathan Fanton, Alan Finberg, Jack Greenberg, Alice H. Henkin, Stephen L. Kass, Marina Pinto Kaufman, Alexander MacGregor, Peter Osnos, Kathleen Peratis, Bruce Rabb, Orville Schell, Gary G. Sick, Malcolm Smith, Maureen White, and Rosalind C. Whitehead.

Addresses for Human Rights Watch

485 Fifth Avenue
New York, NY 10017-6104
Tel: (212) 972-8400
Fax: (212) 972-0905
email: hrwatchnyc@igc.apc.org

10951 West Pico Blvd., #203
Los Angeles, CA 90064
Tel: (310) 475-3070
Fax: (310) 475-5613
email: hrwatchla@igc.apc.org

1522 K Street, N.W., #910
Washington, DC 20005
Tel: (202) 371-6592
Fax: (202) 371-0124
email: hrwatchdc@igc.apc.org

33 Islington High Street
London, UK N1 9LH
Tel: (071) 713-1995
Fax: (071) 713-1800
email: hrwatchuk@gn.apc.org

TABLE OF CONTENTS

ACKNOWLEDGMENTS viii

I. INTRODUCTION x

II. BACKGROUND TO THE CONFLICT 8
    Origins 8
    The Applicable Law 12

III. HUMAN RIGHTS VIOLATIONS BY GOVERNMENT FORCES 16
    Extrajudicial Executions 16
        Dilbagh Singh Uppal (27); Jaswinder Singh, Jasbir Singh, and Arvinder Singh (28); The Family of Ajit Singh (31); Dr. Bhatti (33); Kesar Singh (33); Sukhinder Pal Singh (34); Navtej Singh (35); "Teja" (37); Avtar Singh Khalsa (38); Hardeep Singh and Harjinder Kaur (39)
    Disappearances 41
        Harbhajan Singh (43); Jaspal Singh (43); Lakhwinder Singh (44); Baljinder Singh (44); Jagvinder Singh (45); Disappearances in Jeobala (45); Hardeep Singh (46); Paramjit Singh (48); Amarjit Singh (52); Harjinder Singh (52); Gulab Singh (53); M. Singh and son U. Singh (54); L. Singh (55)
    Torture 55
        B. Singh (60); A. Singh (61); M. Singh (62); S. Singh (63); A. Singh (64); H. Singh (66); S. Singh and Others (67); K. Singh (68); A. Singh (70); P. Singh (71); Village Gobindpura, in Jawarharwala District (73); D. Singh (75); Shahid Kartar Singh Memorial Hospital (76); T. Singh and R. Singh (77); B. Singh (79); A. Singh (79); S. Singh (80); K. Kaur (82); B. Singh (83); K. Singh (84); Ba. Singh (86); S. Kaur and son A. Singh (88); G. Singh and Others (89)

IV. VIOLATIONS OF HUMANITARIAN LAW
   BY MILITANTS 91
      Executions of Civilians 94
         Massacre in Boporai (94); Other Attacks on
         Civilians (95)
      Kidnappings 97
         Abduction and Murder of Jasbir Singh (97)

V. CONCLUSION AND RECOMMENDATIONS 99

Frequently Used Terms

Akali Dal	Sikh political party or parties
ASI	Assistant Subinspector
amritdhari	baptized Sikh
CIA	Criminal Investigation Agency
CRPF	Central Reserve Police Force
DGP	Director General of Police
DSP	Deputy Superintendent of Police
FIR	First Information Report
gurdwara	Sikh temple
lathi	wooden baton carried by police
panchayat	village council
sarpanch	head of the village council
SHO	Station House Officer
SI	Subinspector
SP	Superintendent of Police
SSP	Senior Superintendent of Police

ACKNOWLEDGMENTS

This report was written by Patricia Gossman, research associate for Human Rights Watch/Asia (HRW/Asia). Vincent Iacopino, M.D., Western Regional Representative for Physicians for Human Rights (PHR) and medical director of Survivors International of Northern California contributed substantially to the writing of Chapter III. The report is based largely on research undertaken during a fact-finding mission to Punjab, India, by Ms. Gossman and Dr. Iacopino in October 1992. This research was supplemented by interviews conducted by Human Rights Watch/Asia and PHR in 1993 and 1994, and other documentation about continuing abuses obtained during this time. The report was edited by Sidney Jones, executive director of HRW/Asia, and Cynthia Brown, program director of HRW. It was reviewed by Dr. Iacopino, Susannah Sirkin, deputy director of PHR and Barbara Ayotte, senior program associate of PHR.

We are grateful to those in Punjab and New Delhi who assisted us in our work, particularly the South Asia Human Rights Documentation Centre, the Human Rights Trust and other colleagues in the human rights community in India. Without their advice and assistance, this report would not have been possible. The conclusions we have drawn are the responsibility of HRW/Asia and PHR alone.

I. INTRODUCTION

Nineteen-ninety-three brought to an end one of the bloodiest chapters in India's post-independence history. The decade-long insurgency in the north Indian state of Punjab and the brutal police crackdown that finally ended it cost more than 10,000 lives. Most of those killed were summarily executed in police custody in staged "encounters." These killings became so common, in fact, that the term "encounter killing" became synonymous with extrajudicial execution. Many civilians were also murdered in militant attacks. Hundreds of Sikh men also disappeared at the hands of the police, and countless more men and women were tortured. The price of the government's apparent success against the separatists is the legacy of these abuses: a corrupt and brutalized police force whose resort to murder and torture has been sanctioned by the state as an acceptable means of combatting political violence.

This report documents incidents of torture, extrajudicial executions and disappearances which took place mostly in the first nine months of 1992, at the height of the government crackdown. Throughout the conflict, the government gave widespread publicity to abuses by Sikh militants, and many of the human rights violations described in the report stemmed from deliberate efforts to exact retribution. But there is no indication that the government at the state or federal level since then has made any effort to investigate the abuses committed by its own agents or to prosecute the perpetrators, even though the identity of the latter is well documented. On the contrary, the deliberate use of torture and execution as counterinsurgency tactics was not merely tolerated but actively encouraged by senior government officials.

There are two main reasons for bringing to light cases which happened two years ago or more. The first is to demand full accountability for the actions of officials who in many cases are still in positions of authority and in some cases have been promoted. Unless their involvement in gross human rights violations is understood more widely and punished accordingly, they and their colleagues will not be deterred from using the same methods again, as indeed has happened.

The second reason is to press the government to provide information that might give some belated relief to the families of the victims, who in many cases do not know whether their relatives are alive or dead. In cases where the victims died or were tortured at the hands of the police, some avenue for redress must be provided, both through prosecution of the offenders and through compensation for injuries suffered.

The abuses described in this report, including murder, torture and disappearances, characterized every phase of the government's policy through ten years of conflict in Punjab, as the political confrontation of the early 1980s escalated into near-civil war by 1990.[1] Operation Rakshak ("Protector") II,[2] the counterinsurgency operation that ultimately crushed most of the militant groups by mid-1993, represented the most extreme example of a policy in which the end appeared to justify any and all means, including torture and murder. It was a policy that had been long advocated by senior police officials, in particular Director General of Police K.P.S. Gill, who has had overall authority for counterinsurgency operations. The goal of Operation Rakshak II was to eliminate, not merely arrest, the militant Sikh leadership. Gill also expanded a bounty system of rewards for police who killed known militants -- a practice that encouraged the police to resort to extrajudicial executions and disappearances.

These practices have continued since 1992. Several cases of "encounter" killings, disappearances and torture which occurred in 1993 are documented in this report. Other reports have also documented continuing abuses. In one incident described in the U.S. Department of State *Country Reports on Human Rights Practices*, a twenty-two-year-old farmer, Majinderpal Singh, was picked up by the police on July 12, 1993. On July 14 his family was informed by the police that he would be released within a few days. However, on July 20 the family was told that he had been killed in an "encounter" with police five days earlier. The State Department report also details the case of Kulwant Singh, a lawyer, who was killed along with his wife and child after all three were detained

---

[1] The conflict in Punjab began during Prime Minister Indira Gandhi's tenure (1966-1984). It continued during Rajiv Gandhi's administration (1984-1989), the Janata Dal governments of V.P. Singh (1989-90) and Chandra Shekhar (1990-1991), and the Congress government of P. V. Narasimha Rao.

[2] According to human rights monitors, the government seldom formally announces the end to such operations. Several other police operations, including Operation "Night Dominance" and Operation "Restoration of Peace," partially overlapped with Operation Rakshak II.

I. Introduction

on January 25, 1993, by police from the Ropar police station. Chief Minister Beant Singh reportedly agreed to order an inquiry into the killings but backed down when confronted with police resistance.[3] Amnesty International documents the case of Gurjit Singh, aged twenty-one, who was taken into custody on May 8, 1993 while traveling by scooter with a friend. When the friend and family members inquired at the police station, the police denied arresting Gurjit. On May 11 the parents were told that Gurjit was in custody, but the family was unable to find out where he was being held or the reasons for his arrest.[4] Disappearances and killings of Sikhs thought to be linked to the Punjab conflict also took place outside of Punjab. On May 17, 1993 Punjab police raided an apartment in Calcutta, West Bengal, and shot dead an alleged militant, Lakshmi Singh, and his wife. According to the U. S. State Department, the state government of West Bengal filed a protest with the state government of Punjab, but no disciplinary action was taken against the Punjab police who carried out the killings. Such protests have also been filed from other states. Although he denied the Punjab police were responsible, Director-General of Police K.P.S. Gill admitted that the purpose of such police hit teams was to "trace, identify and kill top militants."[5]

Those who attempted to investigate the abuses were also targeted. Jaspal Singh, the president of the Ropar district branch of the Punjab Human Rights Organization (PHRO), was detained by the Punjab Police on August 16, 1993. He was released on September 1, 1993, only after his case received widespread international and domestic publicity. Other human rights activists have been targeted since 1991, including Ram Singh Biling, district secretary with PHRO, who disappeared after he was detained on January 3, 1992; Jagwinder Singh, a lawyer who disappeared after he was detained on September 25, 1992; Justice Ajit Singh Bains, also with PHRO, who was detained for four months in 1992 and

---

[3] See U.S. Department of State, *Country Reports on Human Rights Practices for 1993*, February 1994.

[4] See Amnesty International, "'An Unnatural Fate': 'Disappearances' and Impunity in the Indian States of Jammu and Kashmir and Punjab," (London: Amnesty International, December 1993), p. 28.

[5] U.S. Department of State, ibid.

Malwinder Singh Malli, another activist with PHRO who was detained for seven months in 1991.

Extrajudicial executions of these suspected militants and sympathizers were carried out as part of deliberate policy conceived by senior police and civil administration officials and implemented by the Punjab police. In their efforts to find and kill the militants, the Punjab police conducted massive search operations, frequently arresting persons who may merely have lived in an area known to be frequented by militant groups or who have belonged to an organization suspected of supporting the militants. In some cases, the police recruited special agents to identify the victims and carry out the killings. Although there was little effort to disguise the nature of these executions, police reports generally claimed the victim was killed in an "encounter" or, occasionally, that he committed suicide to avoid capture. In violation of Indian law, the police usually performed perfunctory post mortems and cremated the bodies in secret. Human Rights Watch/Asia and PHR investigated twenty-one cases of extrajudicial executions, the details of which appear in this report. These represent only a small fraction of those which are believed to have occurred since the launching of Operation Rakshak II.

The Punjab police also engaged in the systematic use of torture. Although the police appear to justify the use of torture as the only way to coerce detainees to confess or to reveal information, in fact the function of torture was to punish detainees and to create a climate of political repression. The practice of torture was facilitated by the fact that detainees were moved frequently from police station to police station without access to the courts, relatives or medical care. Methods included severe beatings, electric shock, suspension by the feet or hands, stretching the legs apart, and crushing the leg muscles with a heavy wooden roller.[6] Family members were frequently detained and tortured in order to reveal the whereabouts of relatives sought by the police. Many such cases are documented in this report.

Those who were most at risk -- who continue to be at risk -- are young Sikh men who were members of one of the Akali Dal political parties, or other political or student groups, or whose relatives or friends were politically active. *Amritdhari*, or baptized Sikhs, those who subscribe

---

[6] These techniques, in particular the stretching of the legs and the roller treatment, are used by police and security forces throughout India, and have been widely documented in Punjab.

I. Introduction

to a strict interpretation of Sikh practices, have also been targeted. The families and acquaintances of suspected militants are particularly vulnerable, as they have been systematically targeted and arrested as a way of forcing suspected militants to identify themselves to the police. Sikhs who previously have been detained during sweep operations, even if they have never been charged, are also at risk. Those who have left Punjab, or who have attempted to relocate to other states in India to escape police persecution, may also be in greater danger because such efforts are construed as conclusive evidence that they are militants.

For the most part, the government of India has responded to criticism about systematic human rights abuses by the Punjab police not by denying the charges, but by countering that the Sikh militants have themselves been responsible for abuses. In fact, senior police and civil authorities in the state and in the central government have acknowledged that the practice of "encounter" killings and other abuses has been widespread, but they have attempted to justify the abuse as the only practical means available for fighting terrorism. To our knowledge, no member of the Punjab police has been subject to criminal prosecution in any case of torture, murder or disappearance.

There is no question that the militants also committed atrocities. From the outset, the militant Sikh organizations deliberately targeted civilians as part of a strategy calculated to terrorize the local population and compel compliance with their demands. The separatist groups flagrantly violated international humanitarian law by killing, kidnapping and assaulting civilians.[7] PHR and HRW gathered direct testimony about some attacks that were apparently designed to terrorize the minority

---

[7] The conduct of insurgent forces is governed not by human rights treaties (to which only states may be parties), but by international humanitarian law, which applies during armed conflicts and is increasingly seen as applicable in situations of internal strife. Despite their separate fields of application, human rights and international humanitarian law share the common purpose of securing for all persons a minimum standard of treatment. For example, both human rights and humanitarian law conventions absolutely prohibit summary executions, torture and other inhumane treatment. The applicability of international humanitarian law does not confer any special status on the militants; nor does it negate the right of the Indian government to prosecute and punish violations of its own criminal laws so long as this is done in compliance with internationally-recognized standards of due process of law.

Hindu population. Victims of these attacks and others have included both Sikh and Hindu civilians, among them Sikh political figures, civil servants, journalists and other community leaders who have opposed the militants' aims. Some of the attacks have occurred outside Punjab in neighboring states and in New Delhi. Militants have also compelled local civilians to provide food and shelter, or to carry out other demands at gunpoint.

Throughout the conflict, the Sikh political leadership remained riven by bitter rivalries and unwilling to distance itself publicly from the militants. By taking up grievances -- including human rights issues -- that Sikh politicians had failed to address, and enforcing their will through terror, the militants early on eliminated virtually all moderate political rivals for power. The groups were also divided among themselves, however, and unable or unwilling to discipline their own forces. By 1992 many of the groups were little more than well-armed criminal gangs, without ideological commitment or military coordination. As a result, they alienated themselves from the civilian population. In mid-1992, as Operation Rakshak II began to yield results in the numbers of militant leaders killed, militant groups struck back by killing the families of police officers. The cruelty of these killings further alienated many in the local population.

The consequences of the Punjab conflict have been far-reaching not only in the state but throughout India. Repressive security legislation enacted in response to the crisis has been used to restrict fundamental rights not only in other areas of conflict, including Kashmir, but against peaceful critics of government policy in Gujarat, Tamil Nadu, Delhi and elsewhere in India.[8] In Punjab, ten years of unfulfilled political reforms and escalating violence in the state fostered a culture of lawlessness and corruption to which the police have become inured; their resort to torture and murder has become institutionalized and accepted at senior official levels of government.

The HRW/PHR team that visited Punjab in October 1992 traveled throughout the state, from the villages around Chandigarh and Patiala in the east to Sangrur, Ludhiana and Amritsar in the center and

---

[8] For example, the Terrorist and Disruptive Activities Act (TADA) enacted in 1985, has been used against Muslims and labor activists in Gujarat. See Amnesty International, *Amnesty International Report 1991* (London: Amnesty International Publications, 1992), p. 114.

I. Introduction

west. The team directly investigated twenty-one cases of extrajudicial executions, twenty disappearances and forty-three cases of torture by the Punjab police. The team also investigated nine killings of civilians by militants and obtained information on thirty-four other killings. During the research mission, HRW and PHR interviewed seventy-one eyewitnesses who provided first-hand information about incidents of abuse. The team also interviewed lawyers, journalists, human rights activists, police officers, members of the state assembly, political party officers, teachers and health professionals, and reviewed *habeas corpus* petitions and other documents on incidents of abuse by the security forces. The PHR researcher, a medical doctor, interviewed and examined thirty-seven persons who had been tortured by the police. In all, HRW and PHR conducted more than one hundred interviews with witnesses and other informed sources, including government officials. In most of the cases investigated, testimony was corroborated by multiple witnesses and physical evidence. While some of those interviewed may have been sympathetic with one side or the other in the conflict, the findings contained in this report are based on HRW and PHR's independent selection of cases and witnesses and analysis of eyewitness testimony, medical examinations and other documentation of the incidents described.

In this report, HRW and PHR have identified many of the police officers and other security personnel whom eyewitnesses have named as participating in or supervising torture or who were responsible for the detention of persons who were subsequently killed in "encounters" or who disappeared. A number of these were also listed in HRW's previous report on Punjab.[9] That they continue on duty in these posts -- or in some cases in more senior positions -- demonstrates that the government has no intention of holding them accountable for the grave human rights violations they committed. On March 26, 1994, India's national Human Rights Commission announced its intent to investigate abuses committed by the Punjab police over the course of the conflict. HRW and PHR recommend that the commission include in its inquiry the cases documented in this report.

---

[9] That report is Asia Watch, *Punjab in Crisis:Human Rights in India* (New York: Human Rights Watch, 1991).

II. BACKGROUND TO THE CONFLICT

Origins

The Punjab conflict began in the early 1980s, after a movement by Sikh leaders for greater autonomy turned violent and extremist factions embarked on a campaign of terror, murdering elected officials, civil servants, and Hindu and Sikh civilians. The groups were led by Sant Bhindranwale, a charismatic Sikh preacher who had been courted by Congress-I[10] leaders hoping to use him to discredit the leadership of the Sikh opposition party, the Akali Dal. The years between 1981 and the Indian army's assault in June 1984 on the holiest of Sikh shrines, the Golden Temple in Amritsar, were marked by protracted negotiations between the government of Indira Gandhi and the Akali Dal leadership.

Control over local river waters was the most important of the Akali demands and was bitterly opposed in the neighboring state of Haryana.[11] In April 1982, the Akali Dal launched a civil disobedience campaign to protest the construction of a dam to divert some of Punjab's river water outside the state. In response, the government broke off talks

---

[10] The Indian National Congress has dominated Indian politics since its founding in 1885, providing most of the organization and leadership behind India's independence movement. Since 1969, the party has suffered a number of schisms; however, the Congress Party (I), for Indira Gandhi, continued to dominate all rival parties. The Congress Party (and the Congress Party (I) after 1969) has won every election since independence except two. After Indira Gandhi's assassination, the party was led by her son, Rajiv Gandhi, who was prime minister from 1984-1989. His assassination on May 21, 1991, ended the Nehru-Gandhi family's control of the party, leaving no clear successor. After the Congress-I victory in the June 1991 elections, P.V. Narasimha Rao became Prime Minister.

[11] Punjab's abundant water supply contributed to the success of "Green Revolution" farming methods which introduced new high-yielding hybrid seeds on a large scale in the state. As a result, Punjab, India's premier agricultural state, soon became its most prosperous. The Akali demands also included the promised transfer of the capital city Chandigarh to Punjab, a Sikh code of personal law, quotas for Sikhs in the military, and the alteration of language in the Indian Constitution that brackets Sikhs with Hindus.

II. Background to the Conflict

with the Akali Dal and banned a number of militant Sikh organizations, many of whose members then retreated to the Golden Temple in the city of Amritsar. By May 1982, the temple complex, which is the size of a small walled city, had become the militants' headquarters, housing several hundred militants and an arsenal of sophisticated weapons.

Protests and civil disobedience campaigns continued, to which the government responded by arresting thousands of Akali leaders and activists under the preventive detention provisions of the National Security Act.[12] Talks between the Gandhi government and the Akali Dal resumed in late 1982 but ended in a stalemate. The government's concern for Congress Party victories in state elections that year and the continuing power struggle between the Akali Dal leaders and the

---

[12] India's National Security Act (1984) permits the detention of persons without charge or trial for up to one year. Under the act, the government may detain persons engaged in behavior "prejudicial to the defence of India, the relations of India with foreign powers, or the security of India." The original Act of 1980 provided for an advisory committee, made up of persons who had been, or were qualified to be, judges of a high court, all of whom were to be appointed by the government. In most cases, the National Security Act of 1984 grants officials four months and two weeks before they are required to notify the advisory board of the grounds for detention. After reviewing the case, the board is to determine whether there is sufficient cause for the person to remain in detention. The National Security (Amendment) Act of 1984 extended from seven weeks to five months and three weeks the period before which the board is required to report to the government its opinion as to whether there is sufficient cause for continued detention. If the board finds the grounds for detention insufficient, the government is to revoke the detention orders and release the detainee "forthwith." Even so, a person may have been detained under the act for nearly six months before that decision is reached. Furthermore, the detainee has no right to appear before the advisory board, and the findings of the advisory board are confidential. A detainee held under the act has virtually no opportunity to file a *habeas corpus* petition until the grounds for detention are communicated to him. Because the amended Act extends the period before which a detainee must be informed of the grounds for his detention from ten to fifteen days, it effectively prolongs the period before which a detainee has recourse to habeas corpus. The amended Act also revises Section 14 (2) of the 1980 National Security Act which had required that a fresh detention order could only be issued if new facts arose. Under the amended Act, detention orders may be renewed on the original grounds, provided the total period of detention does not exceed twelve months.

militants in Punjab undermined the negotiations. Wary of losing ground to Bhindranwale's forces, the Akali Dal began a campaign in April 1983 for the implementation of the Anandpur Sahib Resolution, which called for greater autonomy. In the meantime, the militants stepped up attacks on policemen and civilians. President's rule[13] was imposed on Punjab on October 6, 1983, after a bus was ambushed and six Hindu passengers killed. Further attacks of this kind and the murders of Sikh civilians and suspected militants in alleged "encounters" with security forces set in place the cycle of violence that was to dominate political life in Punjab for the next ten years.[14]

The conflict intensified in 1984 after the Indian army stormed the Golden Temple, which had been turned into an armed fortress by militant forces. Thousands died in the assault, many of them civilians on pilgrimage. In retaliation, on October 31, 1984, Sikh bodyguards assassinated Prime Minister Indira Gandhi, and in the aftermath of her death, mobs slaughtered thousands of Sikhs in New Delhi and other cities across northern India. The connivance of local officials in the massacres and the failure of the authorities to prosecute the killers alienated many ordinary Sikhs who had not previously supported the separatist cause.

On July 24, 1985 Prime Minister Rajiv Gandhi and the Akali Dal leader, Sant Harchand Singh Longowal, signed an agreement granting

---

[13] President's rule is provided for under Article 356 of the Indian Constitution. Under this article, the central government is empowered to dismiss an elected state legislature if the governor, a federal appointee, advises that "governance of the state cannot be carried out in accordance with the provisions of the constitution." The arbitrary manner in which president's rule has been invoked in Punjab and other states has led critics to observe that it has become a tool for purely partisan purposes. See Susan H. Rudolph and Lloyd I. Rudolph, *In Pursuit of Lakshmi: The Political Economy of the Indian State* (Chicago: University of Chicago Press, 1987), pp. 101-102.

[14] As Lloyd Rudolph has observed, "What brought the country to overt civil war ... was Mrs. Gandhi's increasing propensity to speak as if being a terrorist and being a Sikh were one and the same. She coupled this propensity with another, avoiding agreements with moderate Akali Dal leaders. ... By [doing so] she strengthened Bhindranwale's hand, allowing him to capture the community's agenda and tactics. The politics of violence -- of terrorism, assassination and repressive state violence -- was allowed to replace the politics of electoral competition and policy bargaining." Rudolph, p. 42.

II. Background to the Conflict

many of the Sikh community's long-standing demands. The eleven-point accord promised compensation to the families of the victims of the 1984 Delhi riots, and provided that Chandigarh, the capital city, would be transferred to Punjab on January 26, 1986. The accord further provided for a Supreme Court tribunal to adjudicate the dispute between Punjab and neighboring states over water rights, and promised, somewhat vaguely, that the government would take steps to provide Punjab with greater autonomy.

Less than one month later, on August 20, Longowal was assassinated by Sikh extremists who regarded the accord as a compromise and a betrayal. In the Punjab legislature, a splinter party, the United Akali Dal, was launched to protest the accord and boycott state elections scheduled for the end of the year. With an unprecedented voter turnout, however, the Akali Dal swept the elections. The election appeared to signal widespread support for the accord in the Sikh community.

But the promised reforms did not take place. Threatened by angry protests from Hindu leaders in the neighboring state of Haryana, Rajiv Gandhi announced instead a "postponement" of the transfer of Chandigarh. On May 23, 1986, Akali Dal members of parliament resigned in protest to form yet another splinter party aligned with the militants. Violence by extremists escalated, and some groups again established themselves inside the Golden Temple. After that, parts of Punjab were declared "disturbed areas" in which the security forces, including the army, were granted increased powers to shoot to kill.

The newly elected state government's dependence on the support of the central government cost it the confidence of the powerful Sikh religious leaders, and on May 11, 1987, the government collapsed. Ten months later the state assembly was dissolved and president's rule was again imposed. By the end of 1990, violence in the state had surged to unprecedented levels, with nearly 4,000 people reported killed. The murders of more than two dozen candidates and the massacre of seventy-five train passengers on the eve of national elections in June 1991 prompted central government authorities to again cancel the polls in Punjab.

In November 1991, the Director-General of Police (DGP) K.P.S. Gill launched Operation Rakshak, implementing a "catch and kill" policy for suspected militants in order to prepare the ground for elections. The long-postponed elections were finally held in February 1992. Intimidation by militant groups and a boycott by some parties resulted in a turnout of only about 22 percent statewide, and none at all in some rural areas. The Congress-I party formed a government under Chief Minister Beant Singh, but authority for counterinsurgency operations remained with Gill. The crackdown intensified after the elections, and by mid-1993, the counterinsurgency campaign had resulted in the killing of scores of top militant leaders, and the government claimed that "normalcy" had returned to the state. While it is true that most of the militant leaders were killed by the police during this period, the police continued to use terror tactics against the civilian population. The disappearances, torture and extrajudicial killings which accompanied this campaign are the subject of this report.

The Applicable Law

The abuses documented here include major violations of international human rights law, which prohibits the arbitrary deprivation of life under any circumstances. The Government of India is a signatory to the International Covenant on Civil and Political Rights (ICCPR). Article 6 of the ICCPR expressly prohibits derogation of the right to life. Thus, even during time of emergency, "[n]o one shall be arbitrarily deprived of his life."[15] The International Covenant on Civil and Political Rights (ICCPR) also prohibits torture and other forms of cruel, inhuman and degrading treatment. Articles 4 and 7 of the ICCPR explicitly ban torture, even in times of national emergency or when the security of the state is threatened.[16]

The evidence gathered by HRW and PHR indicates that the Punjab police, along with other government forces operating in Punjab, systematically violated these fundamental norms of international human

---

[15] Article 6, International Covenant on Civil and Political Rights.

[16] Article 4 states, "In time of public emergency which threatens the life of the nation and the existence of which is officially proclaimed. . . no derogation from articles 6, 7, 8 (paragraphs 1 and 2), 11, 15, 16 and 18 may be made under this provision." Article 7 states, "No one shall be subjected to torture or to cruel, inhuman or degrading treatment or punishment." International Covenant on Civil and Political Rights, U.N. General Assembly Resolution 2200 A (XXI) of 16 December 1966. India became a signatory on April 10, 1979.

II. Background to the Conflict

rights law. The Punjab police, however, have had overall responsibility for most counterinsurgency operations.

Between 1984 and 1986, and again between 1988 and 1992, Punjab was under direct rule from Delhi. In the absence of an elected state government, the civil administration was under the authority of the governor, a federal appointee. While technically answerable to the governor, the Punjab police in fact operated largely as a parallel administration because of the priority given to fighting the militant movement. Friction between the police and the civil administration over policy in the state left the police less accountable than ever to any civil authority. Even after the elections of February 1992, Deputy General of Police K.P.S. Gill was able to ensure that the new chief minister, Beant Singh, would not interfere with police policy.[17] At the same time, the security forces, particularly the police and the paramilitary forces, were granted sweeping powers under the law to crush the separatist movement and were given protection from prosecution for abuses committed in the performance of duty.[18] Free from accountability to any civil authority, the police increasingly engaged in human rights abuses in the name of fighting "terrorism."

Most of the militant groups which operated in Punjab between 1982 and 1992 were led by followers of Sant Bhindranwale, the Sikh preacher who had been courted first by Congress-I leaders who wanted to discredit that Akali Dal, and then by Akali Dal leaders who wanted the support of his followers. Rifts within the Akali Dal over Bhindranwale's role spawned new militant groups. After Bhindranwale was killed during

---

[17] One long-time correspondent in Punjab told HRW/PHR that because the Congress (I)'s victory in the 1992 elections was based on such a small voter turnout, Beant Singh could not afford to alienate Gill; he needed his support. In 1991, the rift between then Governor Verma and Gill became apparent during a controversy over two incidents of police "encounter" killings. When Verma's home secretary recommended registering criminal cases against the police officials involved, Gill objected, stating that such action would "lead to demoralization and insubordination in the police ranks." Kanwar Sandhu, "New Frictions," *India Today*, November 15, 1990. In January 1991, Verma was transferred to become governor of Himachal Pradesh, and replaced in Punjab by O.P. Malhotra, a former army general.

[18] Both the Punjab Disturbed Areas Act and the Punjab Special Powers Act granted this immunity. For more on this, see Chapter III.

the army assault on the Golden Temple in 1984, the number of groups proliferated. By 1990 they were organized into at least seven major groups -- all theoretically under the authority of one of a number of Panthic Committees which functioned as decision-making bodies and issued instructions. The Panthic Committee headed by Dr. Sohan Singh was historically the most powerful and was supported by the Khalistan Commando Force (Panjwar), Babbar Khalsa, Khalistan Liberation Force (Budhisingwala) and the Bhindranwale Tiger Force of Khalistan (Sangha). Sohan Singh was captured in November 1993. The Panthic Committee headed by Gurbachan Singh Manochahal was supported by the Bhindranwale Tiger Force (Manochahal) and the Khalistan Commando Force (Rajasthani group). The Zaffarwal Panthic Committee was supported by the Khalistan Commando Force (Zaffarwal).[19] In general the groups preferred ambushes, hit-and-run attacks, explosives and assassinations to conventional fighting. Some of the groups operated independently as loosely-organized armed gangs.

Human Rights Watch/Asia and PHR believe that, at least up until mid-1992, the extent of conflict in Punjab rose to the level of application of international humanitarian law, particularly Common Article 3 to the Geneva Conventions, which protects non-combatants in armed conflicts.[20] The militant groups which operated in Punjab between 1980

---

[19] See Monimoy Dasgupta, "Militants are Getting Tired of Fighting: Taksal," Telegraph, February 17, 1991; and ibid, "Doctor May Plan Militants' Strategy," *Telegraph,* April 25, 1991.

[20] Common Article 3 provides, (1) Persons taking no active part in the hostilities, including members of armed forces who have laid down their arms and those placed *hors de combat* by sickness, wounds, detention, or any other cause, shall in all circumstances be treated humanely, without any adverse distinction founded on race, color, religion or faith, sex, birth or wealth, or any other similar criteria. To this end, the following acts are and shall remain prohibited at any time and in any place whatsoever with respect to the above-mentioned persons: (a) violence to life and person, in particular murder of all kinds, mutilation, cruel treatment and torture; (b) taking of hostages; c) outrages upon personal dignity, in particular humiliating and degrading treatment; (d) the passing of sentences and the carrying out of executions without previous judgment pronounced by a regularly constituted court, affording all the judicial guarantees which are recognized as indispensable by civilized peoples. (2) The wounded and sick shall be collected and cared for. See generally Heather A. Wilson, *International Law and*

II. Background to the Conflict

and 1993 flagrantly and routinely violated these provisions of international humanitarian law.

---

the Use of Force by National Liberation Movements (Clarendon-Oxford, 1988), at 45-48, for a review of generally debated criteria and state practice; see also G.I.A.D. Draper, *The Red Cross Conventions* (Stevens and Sons, 1958), at 15-16.

III. HUMAN RIGHTS VIOLATIONS BY GOVERNMENT FORCES

In their efforts to end the insurgency by Sikh militants in Punjab, government forces operating in Punjab committed massive human rights violations. These forces, and the Punjab police in particular, summarily executed civilians and suspected militants in custody,[21] engaged in widespread disappearances and brutally tortured detainees. Those responsible for ordering and participating in these abuses included senior police officials.[22] Those who were aware of the abuses and who condoned them among civilian government officials included officials at the highest levels of the state and central government administration. The HRW/PHR mission to Punjab took place during Operation Rakshak II, and the cases discussed in this report are illustrative of the kinds of abuses which escalated during that campaign. Many more incidents of a similar kind took place in the months that followed our mission, and we have continued to interview witnesses and obtain information about these cases from lawyers, journalists and human rights groups. A number of cases from 1993 and 1994 are included in this report.

---

[21] Article 6 of the International Convention on Civil and Political Rights (ICCPR) prohibits the arbitrary deprivation of life.

[22] The Director General of Police (DGP) is the most senior police officer in the state. Subordinate to the DGP are the Inspector Generals (IG) who generally handle a specific department, such as intelligence. The senior Superintendent of Police (SSP) is subordinate to the IG and the DGP. The SSP has authority over all police matters in his or her district. The Superintendent of Police (SP) answers to the SSP. Lower ranking police officers include Inspectors, Subinspectors, and Assistant Subinspectors. Inspectors and Subinspectors are usually Station House Officers, and have authority over police staff in their station.

III. Human Rights Violations by Government Forces   17

of counterinsurgency operations in the state. No precise figure of the number of those killed in custody is available, but in more than ten years of conflict, the number is almost certainly in the thousands. One police officer told HRW/PHR that he estimated that over a five-year period, 500 people were killed by police from his police station alone. So-called "encounter" killings became so much a part of Punjab's political landscape that few police officials denied the practice existed and many tacitly admitted that it was condoned.[23] As one journalist noted:

> The summary executions policy has the blessings of some key officials at the Centre [i.e. the central government in New Delhi], as borne out by a series of secret communications from Delhi. One such letter of December 30, 1991, from V. G. Vaidya, the special director now promoted as director of the IB [Intelligence Bureau], to Gill came in the wake of SSP [Senior Superintendent of Police] Sanjeev Gupta inadvertently justifying fake "encounters." Wrote Vaidya: "They (district officials) should refrain from even implicitly hinting that they indulge, connive, or approve of anything which is in violation of the law of the land. Their professional compulsions in executive action should not get reflected in their public utterances." The so-called professional compulsions are clearly subverting the law of the land.[24]

In another case, one senior officer's use of police to carry out acts of reprisal caused controversy with the police force itself. After SSP Sumedh Singh Saini narrowly escaped an assassination attempt on August

---

[23] In fact, the killings were so widespread and so routine that they became the subject of black humor by journalists covering the conflict. In a conversation with HRW in March 1993, a senior journalist who had covered Punjab for years recounted a meeting he had had with DGP, K. P. S. Gill, during which Gill threatened a waiter who was too slow in refilling the DGP's beer that he would "have him killed in an 'encounter.'"

[24] Kanwar Sandhu, "Punjab Police: Official Excesses," *India Today*, October 15, 1992, p.33.

29, 1991,[25] that same day police from Saini's station came to the home village of the militant leader of the Babbar Khalsa group and took down the names of five of his relatives who lived in one house. Later that night, gunmen surrounded the house and opened fire, killing three women and a five-year-old child, and then set fire to the house. The next morning, a plainclothes policeman advised the relatives to search for five bodies. The cremation was ordered to be carried out in the presence of the police. Although police officials claimed that the incident was the result of inter-gang rivalry, no group claimed responsibility. On October 17, 1991, Dinesh Kumar reported in the *Times of India* that the SSP of Ropar, Mohammad Mustafa, had

> accused the SSP of Chandigrah, Mr. Sumedh Saini, of ordering the execution of four of [the] family members of top Babbar Khalsa [group] militant Balwinder Singh of Jatana, in retaliation for an unsuccessful attempt by militants to assassinate him. The accusation has been levelled in a confidential letter sent to the Punjab police chief, Mr. D.S. Mangat, in the first week of September....Highly-placed sources in the Punjab government said Mr. Mustafa accused Mr. Saini of despatching three jeep-loads of plain-clothes Chandigarh policemen to Balwinder's native village, Jatana in Ropar district, on the night of 29 August 1991....[T]he Ropar police has officially recorded the crime as committed by "some unidentified persons believed to be militants" to avoid controversy.[26]

Three days after it was published, Mustafa reportedly denied the story.

---

[25] Saini has been identified in many cases of extrajudicial killings, disappearances and torture. See Asia Watch, *Punjab in Crisis*. Although the Babbar Khalsa was originally believed responsible, according to a *Times of India* report, later on, the Khalistan Liberation Force was accused of the assassination attempt. Dinesh Kumar, "Police Accused of Killing Militant's Kin," *Times of India* (Bombay), October 17, 1991.

[26] Ibid.

III. Human Rights Violations by Government Forces

The pattern of "encounter" killings was well established early in the conflict. In most cases, the victim would be detained during police raids on villages or city neighborhoods and tortured for several days before being killed. One police officer who testified to HRW/PHR on condition of anonymity described these raids:

> During my career with the Punjab police, I participated in approximately five raids per day. The orders to conduct the raids were issued by the Senior Superintendent of Police (SSP) or the Station House Officer (SHO). On a typical day, approximately three of the raids were conducted for the purpose of apprehending suspected criminals. These raids were usually conducted during daylight hours. The other two raids typically took place during hours of darkness and were targeted against Sikh families who were suspected of collaborating with armed Sikh militants. The information for these raids was usually provided by paid informants.

Young Sikh men were the most likely to be detained, particularly those who resided in areas known to be militant strongholds or those who belonged to political groups suspected of sympathizing with or supporting the militants. In many of the cases discussed below, the victims had relatives or acquaintances who were suspected to have joined militant groups, and the family members were detained as hostages in order to compel the wanted relative to turn himself in. Detaining relatives was also a way of punishing the family for "harboring" a militant. In most cases these hostages were tortured; in some cases, even after the wanted relative surrendered to the police, the hostages were killed or disappeared.

A policeman we interviewed described the kinds of persons most likely to be arrested:

> Forty percent of those arrested were militants, fifty percent were people suspected of collaborating with militants and ten percent were informants whose identity we wanted to protect by making it look like they were wanted by the police. The fifty people who were

arrested on suspicion of collaborating with militants consisted of two basic types of people -- *amritdhari* (baptized) Sikhs and suspected militant collaborators. Amritdhari Sikhs are considered suspect by the police because of their orthodox observance and practice of the Sikh religion. Police authorities maintain intelligence on all amritdhari Sikhs in a given geographic area. They are routinely characterized as supporters of the movement for an independent state known as Khalistan. When the police have no suspect for a case or need to arrest someone in order to fulfill an arrest quota, amritdhari Sikhs are often the victims. Once an amritdhari Sikh is arrested, it is probable that he will continue to be rearrested after release.

Journalists have also reported that the police singled out amritdhari Sikhs. A report in *India Today* noted:

> The police do appear to attach sinister importance to the partaking of amrit. The State Intelligence Department updates its dossier on amritdharis every month. "Such ludicrous actions only add to resentment," says a police official.[27]

The second group of people targeted are young Sikh men suspected of collaborating with the militants or of being sympathizers with the Khalistan movement. A police officer told us:

> At the time of Operation Bluestar in 1984 when an armed confrontation occurred between Sikhs and government forces surrounding the Golden Temple in Amritsar, a profile was developed of who was considered to be anti-government and pro-Khalistan. Based on that profile, young Sikh men between the ages of eighteen and forty, who have long beards and wear turbans, are considered to be pro-Khalistan. Whenever the police

---

[27] Kanwar Sandhu and Ramesh Vinayak, "Punjab: Area of Darkness," *India Today* (New Delhi), July 15, 1992, p.24.

III. Human Rights Violations by Government Forces

receive a report from an informant or any other individual that Sikh militants have visited the home of a Sikh family, the police are dispatched to raid the home of that family. Pursuant to that raid, any Sikh male who fits the profile described above is arrested.

Police persecution in Punjab has driven a large number of Punjabi Sikhs to seek asylum abroad. According to one of the police officers interviewed by PHR/HRW, those who are denied asylum and returned home face grave risks:

> Another group of individuals who are subject to police scrutiny is anyone who is returned to India after having been deported from the United States, Germany, Canada, England or any other country. Once a deportee reaches an airport in India, he is immediately placed in custody. In Delhi, all returning Sikh deportees are held in the Dhiar Jail. Upon incarceration, a wireless message is sent to Punjab inquiring whether the person is on the police blacklist for political activities. I personally know of an incident in which five Sikh deportees were being held in detention in Bombay after returning from deportation. A wireless message was received at my station, as well as all other stations in Punjab. The message identified the individuals and invited any local station to come get them if they were wanted. I later learned that all five were killed by the authorities in "police encounters."

Our analysis of the testimony of victims and other sources in Punjab has been supplemented by the testimony of more than forty medical evaluations of Sikh political asylum applicants in the United States who alleged that they were tortured in Punjab. All expressed fear of arrest and of being killed by the police if they were to be returned to Punjab.

Where legal remedies exist in Punjab, they proved ineffective in ending the abuses because the police routinely disregarded court orders to produce detainees. A police officer interviewed by PHR/HRW confirmed this practice:

Once a person suspected of harboring militants or of being pro-Khalistan is arrested, he is subjected to detention procedures which circumvent normal police routine. The arrest is not recorded in the daily log which includes the names of all criminals arrested on a given day. There is no official record of the arrest or detention. Instead, the name is placed on a secret "blacklist" which is maintained by the SHO....Even an unsolicited visit by Sikh militants condemns a person to the blacklist....It is also common knowledge that the list is circulated to the SHOs who administer the Punjab police department. Once a person's name is on the police blacklist, he is subject to repeated arrests. If there is any militant activity in the area such as an "encounter," or any activity connected with the pro-Khalistan movement, or even any unsolved criminal activity, a person on the blacklist is subject to rearrest. An individual on the blacklist is considered by police authorities to be a member of the pro-Khalistan movement and is considered to hold anti-government, subversive political views. These individuals are subject to repeated arrests and repeated torture solely by virtue of their identification on the police blacklist.

Detainees were also frequently moved from police station to police station to obstruct the efforts of families and lawyers to locate them. Although the Indian penal code requires that every detainee be produced before a magistrate within twenty-four hours of arrest, the Punjab police consistently ignored the law. Similarly, Indian law requires that every unnatural death be investigated by a magistrate and that a post mortem be performed. The Punjab police routinely have flouted these regulations by performing post mortems not in civil hospitals but on the premises of police stations, and by cremating the bodies of victims before any investigation could take place. In the cases in which bodies were returned to the families, the police usually oversaw the cremation. In most cases of "encounter" killings, the police never acknowledged that a detainee had been in custody. Efforts by local community leaders, including *panchayat* (village council) members and *sarpanches* (heads of the

III. Human Rights Violations by Government Forces

councils), to serve as witnesses to arrests in an attempt to hold police accountable also proved unsuccessful in stopping the killings.

Security legislation which authorizes police to shoot to kill also encouraged abuses. The Armed Forces (Punjab and Chandigarh) Special Powers Act of 1983 and the Punjab Disturbed Areas Act authorize the governor or the central government to declare the whole or any part of the state to be a "disturbed area." During most of the period of conflict in Punjab, the state or significant portions of it were considered disturbed areas. In such an area, the act empowers "any commissioned officer, warrant officer, non-commissioned officer or any other person of equivalent rank in the armed forces" to

> [A]fter giving such due warning as he may consider necessary, fire upon or otherwise use force, even to the causing of death, against any person who is acting in contravention of any law or order for the time being in force in the disturbed area prohibiting the assembly of five or more persons or the carrying of weapons or of things capable of being used as weapons or of fire-arms, ammunition or explosive substances.

Under these laws the security forces are also protected from being held liable for extrajudicial executions.[28] Although the Indian government claims that the laws only require prior sanction for prosecution, in fact prosecutions have been extremely rare, if they have taken place at all.

The Punjab police have also employed undercover agents to identify, kidnap and kill suspected militants. These agents are known as "black cats." Human Rights Watch/Asia and PHR interviewed a police officer whose husband worked undercover as a "black cat" for the police. She said:

> We lived in a civilian locality under undisclosed names. He had a van, and in addition to his official Mauser pistol, he was given four AK-47 guns that were captured

---

[28] Both acts provide, "No suit, prosecution, or other legal proceedings shall be instituted except with the previous sanction of the State Government against any person in respect of anything done or purporting to be done in exercise of the powers conferred [by the Acts]."

from the militants and a bolt-action rifle. He and the others he traveled with dressed in civilian clothes and often had untrimmed beards to make them appear like Sikh militants. They kept their police identification with them, just in case they were accidentally picked up by the regular police. Once they got any information on militants, they would get verbal orders from the SSP to abduct those persons if possible and bring them to the police station for interrogation and torture. If they were unable to abduct someone, then they had orders to shoot and kill. My husband assisted in the abduction of Satwinder Singh ("Toto"), Harpal Singh Babbar, Kawanljit Singh ("Wahuguru"). Among those he helped to kill were Bhinda Kamoke, Lakha from Malaikpur, Kashmir Singh ("Maulvi") and Balwinder Singh.

The government practice of providing cash rewards for police who "eliminate" wanted militants encouraged the police to engage in indiscriminate killings. The existence of police hit lists has been widely reported by Indian and international human rights groups. But because the lists themselves were kept secret, police could easily claim after a killing that the victim was a "wanted terrorist." A police officer explained the use of the "blacklist":

> Once a person's name is on the police blacklist, he faces very severe consequences if he absconds or leaves his home. If a person suspected of pro-militant, pro-Khalistan activities absconds, the police authorities conclusively believe that individual has joined the ranks of armed Sikh militants. If a police patrol discovers that an individual on the police blacklist has left his home, the name is passed on to the SHO for identification as a Sikh militant. Based on the patrol report that the "suspect" individual has absconded, a police order is broadcast by wireless to all police stations in Punjab identifying the "suspect" and requesting that the local station be informed if he is detained....It is commonly understood by police authorities in Punjab that once the name of a suspect individual who has absconded is broadcast over

III. Human Rights Violations by Government Forces

> the wireless, he is considered to be a Sikh militant and is subject to a "shoot on sight" order. Pursuant to police policy, it is acceptable police practice for any officer in Punjab to assassinate in an "encounter" an individual on the list of those who have absconded from their homes.

According to police interviewed by HRW and PHR, the central government created a special fund to finance a network of informants who provided information about militants and those suspected of supporting militants, and to reward police who captured and killed them.

> The reward for each person abducted or killed was about Rs.50,000 [$1,670]. Most of the money was divided among SSP Govind Ram, DSP Harbans Singh and SP Anil Sharma. My husband twice received Rs. 3,000 [$1,000] for the people he killed. My husband was under direct orders of SSP Ram. The SSP was the one who recruited informants and decided who was to be arrested and killed.

The corruption that accompanied this bounty system has been reported in the Indian press. According to a report in *India Today*:

> The rush for claiming cash rewards is turning police into mercenaries. Besides the rewards for killing listed militants (annual outlay for the purpose: Rs. 1.13 crore [$338,000], the department gives "unannounced rewards" for killing unlisted militants. Every week the IGs [Inspectors General] of various ranges send their lists to Additional DG [Director General] (Intelligence) O. P. Sharma. The amount can vary from Rs. 40,000 [$1,333] to Rs. 5 lakh [$16,666].... [T]he operation of the secret fund is only known to a handful of senior police officers -- the DGP, Additional DGs of intelligence and operations, and IG (Crime). Even the home secretary is kept out of

it. Whatever records are maintained are erased after a few weeks.[29]

In many of the cases described below, police officials responsible for the detention of persons who were later killed in custody have been named. Many of these officials were also identified in HRW's previous report on Punjab.[30] The Indian government has repeatedly claimed that it has taken action against police responsible for human rights abuses in Punjab, but in the two and a half years since the HRW report was published, the Indian government has not moved to hold any of these officials criminally liable for murder. Instead, as we noted above, many police officials responsible for numerous "encounter" killings have been promoted to more senior positions.

The Punjab Police have also detained the relatives of suspected militants and others accused of having links to the militants who resided outside Punjab. In some cases, they have bypassed the local police in carrying out arrests; in others, the local police have been involved.[31]

---

[29] Kanwar Sandhu, "Official Excesses," *India Today*, October 15, 1992, pp. 31-32.

[30] See Asia Watch, *Punjab in Crisis*, appendix (pp. 209-210).

[31] Punjab officials have used other state police to carry out personal vendettas. In September 1993, G.S. Bains, the Deputy Commissioner of Hoshiarpur, ordered the Delhi police to detain his daughter, Jaspreet, 23, and her boyfriend, Vipin Gogia, 29, because he did not approve of their plans to be married. On September 15, they filed a petition in the Supreme Court seeking protection for themselves and for Vipin's family in Hoshiarpur. At the hearing, the counsel for the state of Punjab assured the court that Jaspreet and Vipin would be provided adequate protection. Deputy Commissioner Bains failed to appear. On the afternoon of September 19, Jaspreet and Vipin were abducted by the police. They were not released until the Chief Justice threatened to order the dismissal, suspension or transfer of erring police officials of both the Delhi and Punjab police. In ordering the police to produce the couple, the court observed that "the Deputy Commissioner was using the district police to conduct acts of reprisal." The Chief Justice also asked the Punjab government counsel to tell the state's Chief Minister that the court did not consider this case as another "routine Punjab detention." Justice S. Mohan told the Punjab state counsel that the court had its doubt as to whether there was any law and order in Hoshiarpur district. Jaspreet

III. Human Rights Violations by Government Forces

Under DGP K.P.S.Gill, police hit squads have attempted to track down and kill suspected militants in neighboring states and in cities as far away as Bombay and Calcutta. One 1993 case in Calcutta led the state government of West Bengal to file a protest with the state government of Punjab.[32] In another case, Gurbaksh Singh, about 50, was illegally detained on January 22, 1994, by plainclothes policemen from the Operational Cell of the Special Branch of the Delhi police, led by Inspector Khatri. When the police left they took with them a letter which the SSP of Gurdaspur, Punjab, had written in response to a telegram sent by Gurbaksh Singh. The letter pertained to the case of Joginder Singh, the deceased son of Gurbaksh Singh, who had allegedly joined the Babbar Khalsa, a militant Sikh group, in 1991 and was killed in an "encounter" on May 7, 1993. Gurbaksh Singh was released on January 27, after a local human rights group raised his case with officials. No action was taken against any of those responsible for his detention.[33]

Dilbagh Singh Uppal

The death in custody of Dilbagh Singh Uppal, a Bombay city transport worker, in July 1993, prompted the Bombay police to register a FIR against the Punjab police. According to the complaint filed by Dilbagh's brother, Kashmir, on July 3, Dilbagh and Kashmir were picked up by a team of Punjab police led by officer Satwinder Singh. The police had no warrant for their arrest, and the local Bombay police were not informed.

According to Kashmir, the two men were held at an undisclosed place for two days and severely tortured. On July 5, they were made to board the Frontier Mail train out of Bombay where they were again beaten during the journey. Dilbagh was so badly injured because of the

---

and Vipin were subsequently released a few days later, but as of April 1994, no action had been taken against the police officers responsible for their abduction.

[32] *See* U.S. Department of State, *Country Reports on Human Rights Practices for 1993*, February 1994.

[33] Information on this case was provided by the South Asia Human Rights Documentation Centre.

beatings that he could not move without assistance. Kashmir stated that when they approached the city of Shamgarh between the Kota and Ratlam stations, the police threw Dilbagh off the train. The policemen told him that Dilbagh jumped off the train while going to the toilet. According to Kashmir Singh, Dilbagh was too badly injured to have jumped off on his own.

Kashmir Singh was released at Kota railway station, where he waited until Dilbagh's body was brought over for a post mortem.
The body was then transported to Bombay.

After the incident, the Bombay city police commissioner, Amarjeet Singh Samra, ordered that the Punjab Police be accompanied by a local police officer whenever they operated in the city. As of April 1994, no police officer had been prosecuted in connection with the incident.

Jaswinder Singh, Jasbir Singh, and Arvinder Singh

On July 12, 1992, Jaswinder Singh, aged thirty, his brother-in-law, Jasbir Singh, and Jaswinder's son, Arvinder, aged three, all residents of Dhulkot in Ambala district, were shot by the Punjab police as they were returning home by car. As they neared Dhulkot, a police car began following them. When their car skidded on the turn from the main road onto the village road, Jaswinder, Jasbir and Arvinder got out of the car. Seconds later the police car arrived, and five policemen got out of their car and shot all three as they ran across the road. Jaswinder and the child died immediately; Jasbir died on the way to the hospital. The other bodies were returned to the families after a post mortem at the civil hospital.

A number of residents of Dhulkot witnessed the incident or saw the bodies immediately afterwards. B. Singh told us that when he reached the site of the shooting, the policemen had pulled Jasbir's and Jaswinder's bodies out of the irrigation ditch; B. saw the body of the child still lying in the ditch. Jasbir, who had been shot in the chest and abdomen, was still alive, but unconscious and breathing rapidly. B., along with two other men from the village, told us that they got into the van to prevent the police from planting weapons on the bodies. They accompanied the police as they took Jasbir to the civil hospital; the bodies were taken to the morgue.

J., who witnessed the shooting, stated that he saw the men raise their hands in surrender before they were shot. He said that when he

III. Human Rights Violations by Government Forces

asked the police why they were killing the men, the police responded, "These boys are terrorists and there are prizes of 10 lakhs [Rs. 1,000,000 or $32,000] on their heads." J. identified the police officer in charge as Subinspector Dhyar Singh, of the Criminal Investigation Agency (CIA) staff, Ambala, who was accompanied by four plainclothes Punjab policemen from the Patiala police station. Dhyar Singh was well-known to local residents, some of whom stated they had known him for fifteen years.

R. told us that he was at a local factory that day when he heard a burst of gunfire that lasted a few minutes. He saw people running and followed them. When he reached a spot about 300 yards down the road, he saw the body of his next-door neighbor, Jaswinder Singh, and Jaswinder's son lying in a police van. Jasbir Singh, who was injured, was also in the van. Two villagers were sitting with Jasbir in the van: S. Singh and B. Singh.

Ja., Jaswinder's uncle, was at home in the center of the village when the shooting occurred. He heard two bursts of gunfire, then five minutes later learned that his nephew had been shot. By the time he arrived at the site, a police jeep carrying uniformed police was there. Ja. saw that the superintendent, K.P. Singh, who was in civilian clothes, was preventing people from going near the site. However, Ja. insisted on seeing the bodies, and when he reached the spot he saw the three lying face up. He saw that Jaswinder had a bullet wound just above the right eye, and multiple wounds in his chest and right arm. The police asked him to identify the body and then took him over to the van, where he identified Jasbir. He told us that both men were unarmed.

In the presence of the villagers who had gathered there, the police searched Jasbir, the two bodies and the car, and on the insistence of the village elders, the police certified that no weapons had been recovered. According to a human rights lawyer, the certification was placed in the case file. The villagers recovered a large number of bullet casings that had been fired from the police guns; this too was entered in the police record.

After the police had removed Jasbir and the bodies, some villagers remained to guard the car until SHO Surjit Singh, of the Sadar Ambala police station arrived, and then insisted that he also verify that the victims had no weapons. Members of the panchayat and the sarpanch came with the SHO to ensure that he did so, and the police provided a copy of the SHO's statement to this effect to Jaswinder's mother and brother.

The villagers then blocked the main road until midnight to demand that the police responsible be brought before them. The SHO ordered them to disperse, but they refused. The five policemen were brought in front of the villagers at 4:00 P.M., but they remained inside the police van where the villagers could not easily see them. The protest continued until 7:00 P.M., when the policemen were again brought and the villagers identified them as the five who had shot Jaswinder, Jasbir and Arvinder.

The next day, July 13, the deputy speaker of the state assembly, Sumev Chand Bhat, came to the village and the police announced that families of the victims would each receive Rs. 20,000 [$670] compensation. On July 14, Chief Minister Bhajan Lal announced that the compensation would be raised to Rs. 100,000 [$3,350] for Jasbir and Jaswinder, and Rs. 50,000 [$1,675] for the child, to be paid to the families within a week.

A case was registered against the police. In their bail application, the police contended that they were falsely identified. They did not claim to have recovered any arms on the victims, or that Jasbir or Jaswinder opened fire. The police were arrested on July 15, 1992, on a charge under Section 302 (murder) of the Indian Penal Code (IPC) that was later converted to 304A (causing death by negligence or culpable homicide not amounting to murder) on July 29. They remained in remand for fifteen days before being released on bail. According to the human rights lawyer representing the families of the victims, after the police were released, the case against them went "nowhere." To our knowledge, none of the policemen has been prosecuted for the killings.

The post mortem examinations were performed on July 13 at the Civil Hospital in Ambala. Dr. Iacopino of PHR reviewed copies of the post mortem reports. The examination of Jasbir's body revealed a total of six entrance and exit wounds to the chest, abdomen and buttocks. The detailed descriptions of the wounds indicated that they were produced by firearms. The examination of Jaswinder Singh's body revealed a total of thirteen entrance and exit wounds to the head, chest, abdomen and extremities. Jaswinder's three-year-old son, Arvinder Singh, had a total of four entrance and exit wounds to the head and face. The post mortem wound descriptions of all three victims indicated that many of the shots came from behind them.

III. Human Rights Violations by Government Forces

According to an article about the incident which was published in *India Today*, the police had been told by an informer that Jaswinder was a militant named Nirvair Singh. "The police, ostensibly in a rush to claim the reward, opened fire."[34]

The Family of Ajit Singh

M. Singh, aged ninety, a resident of Kilibodla in Ferozepur district, told us that at about 4:45 P.M. on October 7, 1992, he saw Jaginder Singh, a resident of the nearby village of Sood, running down the road toward M.'s house, followed by fifteen police in two jeeps, led by Subinspector Balkar Singh. Jaginder ran into the courtyard, turned and shot SI Balkar Singh and SI Jarnail and then escaped. M. described what happened next:

> The other police surrounded the house and made everyone come out into the courtyard: Ajit Singh, aged forty-five, his wife, Lakhwinder Kaur, aged forty-five, Ajit's mother Iqbal Kaur, aged eighty, Ajit's daughter-in-law Manjit Kaur, aged twenty-five, Ajit's younger brother's wife Jaswinder Kaur, aged forty-five, and her two sons, Sukhwinder Singh, aged twenty-one, and Rajinder Singh, aged fifteen. Other police reinforcements completely surrounded the area and blocked all the roads.

J. Kaur, aged eighteen, who lived nearby, told us:

> The police beat Rajinder and Sukhvinder with their rifle butts for about ten minutes. I heard the police say to bring the women, and they beat them too. I could hear them screaming for about ten minutes. Then I heard a burst of gunfire at about 7:15 P.M. and I saw flames coming up near the tree beside the house. About forty-five minutes later I heard three explosions. Then I heard nothing more. The next morning at 6:00 A.M., Devraj Sharma of the Zira police station came to our house and

---

[34] Kanwar Sandhu, "Official Excesses," p. 30.

accused us of giving shelter to the militants. He said, "We have already killed seven members of that family and now we are going to shoot you."

Assistant Subinspector (ASI) Lekraj Singh of Makhu police station then took J. Kaur and K. Singh, aged eighty, to the Makhu police station, where the police had already taken Ajit Singh's granddaughter, Narinder Pal Kaur, aged three. He ordered them to take the child home and to go to the Zira police station and identify the bodies of the other family members. J. Kaur and K. Singh were taken to the police station in a police jeep, but when they arrived, the other policemen standing outside would not allow them to go in. The sarpanch of Kilibodla, Harpinder Singh, met them there at about 10:00 A.M. The police allowed him in to see the bodies, and then at about noon J. Kaur and K. Singh were permitted to take the bodies. J. Kaur described the injuries:

> Rajvinder Singh's left arm was broken and the bone was protruding. He had bullet wounds in his chest and abdomen. Ajit Singh had bullet wounds in the chest and blood on his shoulders. Manjit Kaur had bullet wounds to the head, and her knees appeared to have been crushed. Jasvinder Kaur's head was swollen and she had bullet wounds to her chest and legs. The other bodies also had bullet wounds in the chest and abdomen. Lakhwinder's arm had been badly burned and the hands of all of other the bodies had also been burned.

When HRW examined the site on October 13, 1992, a rope and chain which were wrapped around the tree in the courtyard were dangling from one of the branches. The wall on the outside of the house had been recently burned, and charred skin was visible on the ground near the wall. There were also bullet holes in the gate. Inside the house, trunks had been broken open and the television had been smashed.

According to a local journalist, who visited the site soon after the killings, the police claimed that the family had been killed in cross-fire.

III. Human Rights Violations by Government Forces

Dr. Bhatti

J., a resident of Manauli, told us that one night in July 1992, at about 10:30 A.M., two police vans stopped on the main road. One man in civil dress asked for directions from a nearby shop to a clinic run by Dr. Bhatti. A number of Central Reserve Police Force (CRPF) officers and commandos then took up positions around the clinic. Three of the officers entered the clinic and asked Dr. Bhatti to treat one of their men, who they said was ill in the van. Dr. Bhatti asked for details of symptoms and then prepared an injection and told his assistant to go to the man, but the police insisted that Dr. Bhatti come himself.[35] By this time a number of villagers had gathered at the clinic. They reported that Dr. Bhatti hesitated but went to the corner where the van was waiting.

N., aged fifty, a farmer and resident of Manauli, told HRW/PHR that he was standing outside at the time and could see a person sitting in the van with his face covered by a hood. The police asked the hooded man if he could identify Dr. Bhatti. When the man nodded, the police told Dr. Bhatti to get into the van. When he hesitated, they pushed him in and the van drove off.

Afterwards, Dr. Bhatti's mother and wife inquired at the local police station but were not able to get any information about what had happened to Dr. Bhatti. Three or four days later, a report appeared in the local papers that the "dreaded militant," Dr. Jagtar Singh Bhatti, had been killed in an "encounter" with the police. The photograph that was published with the reports was that of Dr. Bhatti. The residents said that the police had not come to the village before, and that they were not aware of Dr. Bhatti treating any outsiders or militants.

Kesar Singh

Kesar Singh, aged twenty-three, a photographer and a resident of Chhajli village, in Sangrur district, was arrested by the Punjab police on January 16, 1992. Shortly after Kesar had returned from meeting his brother D. at the State Bank in Sangrur at about 5:30 P.M., the police surrounded his house. The police threatened family members and neighbors who had gathered, saying they would shoot anyone who tried to intervene. They then tied Kesar's hands behind his back with his

---

[35] It is not uncommon for police to compel the services of doctors in this way.

turban, pushed him in the van and drove off. At about 7:00 A.M. the next day, Kesar's brother D., accompanied by a local teacher who was acquainted with the Station House Officer (SHO), went to see the SHO at the Sunam police station. The SHO told them that Kesar had not been arrested by the Sunam police but told them to come back and he would see whether he could find out what had happened. In the evening D., together with Baldev Singh Mann, a former minister, met with the SSP during a conference of area police officers. All of the officers denied having Kesar in custody, and the SSP told them, "I do not delay matters, I make a decision on one side or the other: either we have Kesar or he does not exist anymore."

On the morning of January 18, D. heard that Kesar had been detained by the Dharn police along with a man named S. Singh from the nearby of village of Kattu. A short time later the local newspapers reported that two unidentified militants traveling on a scooter were shot dead by police after they opened fire at a police checkpoint. D. went to see the DSP for Barnala district who denied that the two men had been in custody. Then D. went to the civil hospital at Barnala and spoke with the doctor who had done the post mortem on the bodies. The doctor described two men whose ages and general descriptions matched those of Kesar and S. D. also went to the site of the alleged "encounter," and the villagers there told him that one of the men was from Kattu and the other from Chhajli. When the family asked for Kesar's body, the police told them it had already been cremated and that they would not hand over the ashes unless the family agreed to sign a statement saying that Kesar had left home two years ago. The family agreed, and the ashes were returned.

Sukhinder Pal Singh

Sukhinder Pal Singh, aged twenty-five, a resident of Dakha, was reported as being killed in an "encounter" shortly after being taken into custody by the Punjab police on September 30, 1992. Sukhinder had returned home from the milk plant where he worked that evening when, at about 7:00 P.M., seven or eight policemen from the Dakha police station came to his house and asked him to identify himself. He told them his name. Then the police asked his mother who owned the house, and she gave them the name of her husband. Then they searched the house, but took nothing. They left, taking Sukhinder with them in the van.

III. Human Rights Violations by Government Forces

The next day, Sukhinder's mother went with the village sarpanch to the Dakha police station where she was able to speak to Sukhinder and give him some food. She was able to see him there every day for the next five days, although she could only meet with him in the presence of the SHO. On October 1, his sister met with Sukhinder. On October 3 and 5, his mother was permitted to see him only from a distance. On October 6, the constable on duty refused to let her see him, saying that there was no officer present who could let her in.

On October 7, a police report published in the *Indian Express*, *Tribune*, and the Punjabi Daily *Ajit* stated that two "militants," Sukhinder Pal Singh and Navtej Singh, had been killed in an "encounter" with police from the Dakha and Sidhar police stations near the Changna canal bridge, about three kilometers away. The press notice had been issued by SSP Swaran Singh of the Jagraon police station.

After this, the sarpanch and other prominent residents of the village went to the Dakha police station where they were told that the bodies of the two men had already been cremated at Goghat in the city of Ludhiana. The sarpanch told us:

> When we went to the police station to ask for the remains, SHO Joginder Singh asked us, "Of what use are the dead bodies to you?" After we insisted, Joginder Singh told us that the bodies had been cremated in Goghat. So we went with Sukhinder's mother and sister to Goghat and to another cremation ground but the caretakers at both places told us that no dead bodies had been brought from Dakha.

Sukhinder had never been arrested before, nor had anyone else in the family.

Navtej Singh

H. Singh, aged fifty-one, an electrician and resident of Dakha, told HRW/PHR about the killing of his son Navtej, aged twenty-five, who was also an electrician.[36] In April 1992, H. was picked up by police from the Sadar police station in Ludhiana who were looking for Navtej.[37] H. was released after Navtej reported to the police station. Navtej was released after four days and was not tortured during that time. After that he went to live with his maternal grandparents in another city.

Navtej returned to his village just before a friend's wedding scheduled for October 3, 1992. On the night before the wedding, the police led by DSP Harbans Singh and Inspector Gurdeep Singh surrounded the house of the wedding party where Navtej was staying. They arrested nine young men: Navtej, Yadvinder Singh, Charan Singh, Kamal Singh, Amardeep Singh, Jagjit Singh, Baljinder Singh, "Kaka," the son of Ravail Singh and "Puppy," the son of Labh Singh. H. witnessed their arrest as did many of the villagers and wedding guests. The police tied the hands of the nine men with their turbans, slapped and insulted them in the presence of the wedding guests and then took them to the Dakha police station. H. followed them to the police station but was not permitted inside. Amerdeep, Kamal and Jagjit were released later that day, because of the wedding in their family, but told to report to the police station later.

H. continued to ask about Navtej's whereabouts but was unable to obtain any information. However, on October 6, one of the employees at the police station confirmed that the men had been taken there the night they were arrested. On October 7, the newspaper *Ajit* published a police report stating:

> According to a correspondent from Jagraon, in Jagraon police district, near village Dakha, two militants, Sukhinder Singh and Navtej Singh were killed at the hands of the security forces. This incident took place this morning. A revolver, a gun and some cartridges were recovered from the spot.

---

[36] Navtej had been detained on two other occasions before he was killed, once in 1990 and again in April 1992. In both cases, his father was picked up in order to force Navtej to come in to the police station for questioning.

[37] H. was tortured while in police custody. For more on his case, see p.66.

III. Human Rights Violations by Government Forces 37

When H. inquired at the police station, he was informed that Navtej's body had already been cremated and that he could collect the ashes from a crematorium in Ludhiana. However, when H. went to the place, the staff at the crematorium Ludhiana denied receiving Navtej's body. Police at Dakha Police Station subsequently said they had no further information. Before this incident, Navtej Singh's father had once been detained at CIA staff headquarters in Ludhiana and told to produce Navtej. Navtej was detained at that time but later released.

"Teja"

On July 29, 1992, at about 4:00 A.M., about fifteen policemen came to the house of Avtar Singh Khalsa in the village of Fatehgarh, in Sibian district. When C. Kaur opened the door, the police asked her how many men were in the house. When she replied that there were none, they asked her where "Teja" was. She said that he had gone to Delhi to get his passport renewed and that he would return in three or four days. Then they told her that when he came back he should report to the CIA staff headquarters in Jagraon.

Later that day, at about 2:00 P.M., a large deployment of police led by DSP Bhagwan Singh Sodhi of the Jagraon police station came to the house and demanded that C. Kaur hand over arms and ammunition they said were hidden in the house. When she told them there were none, the police dug up the courtyard and the land around the house. The police claimed that they had received a tip that there were weapons hidden in the house. When she repeated that she did not know about it, the DSP told the police to make her tell them where the arms were hidden. They took her into the house and tied her hands behind her back. One policeman pulled her by her hair while two others pulled her legs apart. When the DSP came into the room, he said to the police, "If she won't tell, take her to station and she will tell there." At the police station, they brought out the young man whom they claimed had told them about the arms. The man told her the police had beaten and tortured him and that he was afraid they would do it again. She then told police that she thought some weapons might have been hidden in the field.

The police brought her and the boy back to the house and searched the field until they found one machine gun. They took it, and brought C. Kaur and the boy back to the police station. Then they picked up an acquaintance named B. Singh, a relative named Bl. Singh, and C.

Kaur's son, G. Singh., and brought all of them to the Jagraon police station. B. and Bl. were released the next day on the condition that they produce Teja. C. Kaur and her son remained in the police station.

On August 1, at about 5:00 P.M., Bl. and B., along with several prominent persons from their village and surrounding villages, handed Teja over to the CIA staff in Jagraon. After she and her son saw Teja, they were set free. The next day, when she came to collect her gold earrings and watch from the police, she obtained permission from the guard to talk to Teja, and he told her that he had been badly tortured with the roller[38] and had also been beaten with *lathis* (wooden batons) all over his body. His face was bruised. He told her she should try to find some influential person to save him or else he would be killed.

After that she went to the police station nearly every day for seventeen days, during which time the police continued to promise her that Teja would be released. They did not permit her to see him again. On August 18, the sarpanch told her that he had learned from the DSP that Teja had been killed. The next day a police press report published in the local newspapers said that three militants had been killed. Two were identified as Avtar and Jagjit; the third was referred to as "unidentified." A machine gun similar to the one found in the field was alleged to have been recovered from the militants. C. Kaur learned that the bodies had been cremated at the grounds on Raikot Road in Jagraon. When she went there, the grounds keeper told her that all three men had been cremated in the same pit, and he gave her the ashes.

Avtar Singh Khalsa

The police also went to the residence of Teja's brother, Avtar, and when they were told that he was not at home, they demanded that Avtar be produced at the police station. The family sent a message to Avtar, who was visiting a relative, telling him to come home. On July 31, Avtar,

---

[38] This method of torture involves rotating a heavy wooden log or iron pipe over the detainee's legs, crushing the muscle tissue. Police frequently stand on the roller to increase the pressure. The practice gained notoriety during the Emergency of 1975-77, following widespread publicity about the death of a detainee who had been subjected to continual torture with the roller. See Amnesty International, *Amnesty International Report 1977* (London: Amnesty International Publications, 1978), p.183.

III. Human Rights Violations by Government Forces 39

accompanied by members of the panchayat, went to the fields and pointed out where several rifles were hidden. Then he surrendered to the CIA staff. The panchayat leaders went to the police station every day, but the police refused to allow them to see Avtar. On August 19, a police press report was published in the local newspapers that said Avtar had been killed in an "encounter."

Hardeep Singh and Harjinder Kaur

On August 11, 1992, at about 5:30 A.M., SHO Darshan Singh of the Dehlon police station and Constable Avtar Singh of the Latala police post, together with about seven other policemen, detained A. Singh, a resident of the village of Latala, his wife, N., A.'s cousin Hardeep Singh and several other men from the village.[39] At the time that A. and the other men were picked up, Hardeep Singh was already lying unconscious in the police van. A. stated that by the time they reached the Sudhar police station, Hardeep's breathing was labored, and he was unable to drink water. A. told the constable on duty that he should call a doctor, and four policemen carried Hardeep away.

At 7:00 P.M. the other detainees were put in two lock-ups, with about eighteen men in each. A third lock-up was screened with black cloths. At 8:00 P.M., when the detainees were taken out of the two lock-ups to be fed, no one left the third lock-up. In the morning, the black cloths were removed, and A. saw that the third lock-up was now empty. The police ordered some of the detainees to wash it out. After that, the detainees were divided into all three lock-ups. On August 13, when A. asked the police about Hardeep, SHO Darshan Singh told him Hardeep had been taken to the state of Uttar Pradesh, over 100 miles away, to point out arms caches. A. was released on August 19 without ever being told why he had been detained. Hardeep was not released, and A. was not told what had happened to him.

After Hardeep was arrested, his father, M. Singh, went to Pakhowal to see the local Member of the Legislative Assembly (MLA), Darsel Jodha. Together they went to the Dehlon police station and met with SHO Darshan Singh, who assured them that Hardeep and A. would

---

[39] A. was tortured before being put into the police van. For a discussion of this, see p.79.

be released at 6:00 P.M. But at 6:00 P.M., the police said that the men could not be released.

Hardeep's uncle, who lives near Hardeep, stated that on August 11, he saw the police surround Hardeep's house. When he came out to see what was going on, the police threatened to shoot him if he tried to intervene. He described what he saw:

> The police had tied Hardeep's hands behind his back and were hitting him with their rifle butts and kicking him. His wife, Harjinder Kaur, had fallen down and I saw the police pick her up and put her on a cot. They poured buckets of water over her body, then they started beating her with their rifle butts. As she was screaming, one policeman kicked her in the throat with the heel of his boot; another one kicked her in the abdomen. The other police stretched Hardeep's legs out to the sides and kicked him in the chest and abdomen. The inspector was supervising both beatings. Then the police dragged Hardeep out of the yard. Harjinder Kaur was left on the cot. When the police left I ran to get the panchayat.

C. Kaur, a neighbor, stated that as soon as the police left, she and another neighbor went to Harjinder Kaur and untied her hands, which had been tied with her *dopatta* (scarf).

> Harjinder Kaur was conscious and she screamed with pain when we picked her up. We tried to give her a spoonful of milk and some water, but she vomited. We brought the village doctor, and he told us to take her to the hospital as her condition was serious. We got to the Ahmedgarh Mandi township hospital in Kunban Lal some time after 3:00 P.M.; Harjinder Kaur died about 4:00 P.M. When we tried to take her body back, the doctor notified the police, who told us we could not take the body until we signed a statement saying that she had been injured by a buffalo falling on her. We refused, and police from the Dehlon police station took the body away from us. The post mortem was conducted at the civil hospital in Ludhiana.

III. Human Rights Violations by Government Forces

The next day, demonstrations were held outside the office of the SSP and district collector (local official) in Ludhiana. M. approached senior police officials, who repeatedly assured him that A. and Hardeep would be released before the last rites were held for Harjinder Kaur on August 20. After A. was released on August 19, the MLA, Darsel Jodha, met with SSP Swaran Singh from Jagraon and asked him about Hardeep. The SSP told him that Hardeep had run away. Jodha replied, "How could he run away? If he is dead, you should tell us." The SSP replied, "What do you want me to say? You should understand."

According to a report in *India Today*, the post mortem report attributed Harjinder's death to "hemorrhage and shock as a result of extensive injuries" but noted that a buffalo was the probable cause. The report also noted that local villagers reported that Darshan Singh often said, "I can't digest my food till I've knocked off a person or two." As a result of publicity about the case, SHO Darshan Singh was demoted.[40]

Disappearances

The forced "disappearance" of persons taken into police custody increased dramatically in the latter years of the Punjab conflict, and particularly during Operation Rakshak II. As in the cases of "encounter" killings, the police routinely obstructed legal efforts to have the detainee produced in court. In most cases, they simply denied that the detainee was ever in custody. In others they claimed that the victim "escaped" while being taken to look for hidden weapons or being transferred to another police station. Thus, unlike "encounter" killings where the families often receive the ashes, the families of the disappeared have never been able to end their search and perform the last rites for their relatives. Disappearances can be a form of extrajudicial execution. The number of disappearance cases in Punjab is not known but may be as high as several thousand.

The first case discussed below illustrates the pattern of disappearances in Punjab. We first interviewed the principal witness, Hari Singh, about the 1989 disappearance of his son, Hardial Singh, in

---

[40] Tarun J. Tejpal, "Punjab Police: Dangerous Overkill," *India Today*, September 15, 1992, p. 31.

December 1990.[41] When we returned to Punjab in October 1992, Hari Singh told us that he had spent the two years between our visits trying to follow up every possible lead that might help him locate his son or learn what had happened to him, but found no trace of him.

Hardial Singh had been on his way to a court hearing at 10:00 A.M. on August 18, 1989, when he was forced into a police van by Harbans Singh, the SHO of the CIA staff, and three armed constables, just as he and his father were about to board the bus at the bus stand in Taran Taran. Hari Singh never saw his son again. When he got to the CIA staff headquarters in Taran Taran, he asked SHO Harbans Singh why Hardial had been arrested, Harbans acknowledged that Hardial was in custody but would not let Hari Singh see him. Three days later, the SHO told Hari that Hardial was not in custody. From that point on, SHO Harbans Singh continued to deny ever having arrested Hardial. In November 1990, Hari Singh was told that higher officials were making an inquiry. At the same time, Harbans Singh was promoted to inspector.

Hari learned nothing until June 1992, when he was told by a former detainee that his son had been held by the 33rd battalion of the CRPF. On July 20, Hari was summoned by police from the Naushera Panual police post, who asked him where Hardial was. He told them he believed he was in police custody. The police told him that the superintendent (SP) had ordered an inquiry into the case. The head constable, Lakhe Singh, recorded Hari's statement but at the time we interviewed him, there had been no other development in the inquiry or news of his son.

Jagtar Singh

Jagtar Singh, a milk vendor and resident of the village of Sidhupur Kalan in Fategarh Sahib district disappeared after being arrested on August 24, 1993. Jagtar and his brother were returning home after work when they were stopped by police from the Kharar police station who made Jagtar get into their van with a license number PB-12-1284 and then drove off. His brother returned home with Jagtar's bicycle and milk cans.

Over the next two weeks, Jagtar's family members and friends met the DSP of Kharar, Harinder Singh, and the SHO, both of whom

---

[41] Asia Watch, *Punjab in Crisis*, pp. 96-97.

III. Human Rights Violations by Government Forces

denied that Jagtar was in custody. A neighbor who had been in the police station saw Jagtar there on August 24.

On September 14, a delegation of thirty panchayats from the district met with Jagmohan Singh, a minister in the state government who told them to come to a regional conference on September 20 in the town of Morinda at which police officials from the three districts of Ropar, Fatehgarh Sahib and Khanna would be present. Some one hundred panchayats attended the meeting and demanded Jagtar's release. The police officials present announced that the SP of Ropar district had been ordered to undertake an inquiry into the case. As of March 1994, the family has been unable to obtain any information from the Ropar SP about the results of the inquiry and Jagtar's whereabouts remain unknown.

Harbhajan Singh

Harbhajan Singh, a resident of Hirapur village in Jalandhar, disappeared after being arrested on July 2, 1993. According to an affidavit filed by his wife, Ravinder Kaur, the police, some of whom were in uniform, came to the house at about 4:00 A.M. They refused to tell her why they were arresting Harbhajan. Over the next several days, Ravinder Kaur and the village panchayat made inquiries at local police stations but were unable to obtain any information about Harbhajan. On September 16, she filed an application with the SSP of the Jalandhar police station, on the basis of which the SSP filed a FIR against the police. However, as of April 1994, nothing had been learned about Harbhajan's whereabouts and no action taken against those responsible for his disappearance.

Jaspal Singh

Jaspal Singh, aged thirty-six, a farmer in Baina Bulund, Fatehgarh Sahib district, was arrested from his farm in the village of Noorpura on the morning of February 18, 1993. According to witnesses, three unmarked police jeeps arrived at the farmhouse. The police searched the premises, and then tied Jaspal's hands behind his back, forced him into one of the jeeps and left. The police did not tell the family why they were arresting Jaspal.

Jaspal's father repeatedly made inquiries at the Sangrur, Fatehgarh and Patiala police stations and met with the SSP but was unable to obtain any information about the whereabouts of his son. He was able to determine, however, that no case had been filed against Jaspal. He also met with DGP K.P.S. Gill, who told him, "No one named Jaspal Singh has ever been taken into police custody from the village of Baina Buland." Since the, the family has had no further information about Jaspal's fate or whereabouts.

Lakhwinder Singh

Lakhwinder Singh, aged thirty-five, a police constable with the Majitha police station, disappeared after being taken into custody on January 17, 1993. At the time, Lakhwinder had been posted as a security guard to S. Sewa Singh, the sarpanch of the village of Liddar. S. Sewa Singh and Lakhwinder were arrested by police from the Verowal police station in Khadur Sahib, in district Taran Taran. S. Sewa Singh was released on January 25, but although Lakhwinder's father and brother saw Lakhwinder at the police station, he was not released. The family inquired at other police stations and met with the SSPs of Taran Taran and Majitha, but they obtained no further information about Lakhwinder's whereabouts.

Baljinder Singh

On October 3, 1992, at about 2:30 A.M., police from the Dakha police station again raided the house of R. Singh in the village of Dakha.[42] SHO Joginder Singh led the operation. When R. saw the police, he ran away. His younger brother, Baljinder, also tried to escape but was caught by the police who then tied his hands behind his back and took him to the police station. The police told the family he would be released only if they turned in R. The mother was permitted to see Baljinder on October 4. On the same day, SHO Joginder Singh brought two other detainees, Sukhinder Pal Singh and Navtej Singh,[43] before her and told her, "They have named your boy, and I want him." She said that Navtej was in such bad shape that he had to crawl into the room. The next time she came back to see Baljinder, the jail guard told her he

---

[42] For more on the earlier arrest and torture of R. Singh, see p.77.

[43] For more on the killings of these men, see p.34, 35.

III. Human Rights Violations by Government Forces

was not there, and she was unable to obtain any more information about what had happened to him.

Jagvinder Singh

Jagvinder Singh, aged twenty-five, a lawyer and resident of Laxmi Nagar, Kapurthala, disappeared after being picked up from his home by uniformed Punjab police on September 25, 1992. According to witnesses, the police officials told him that, M.K. Tiwari, the SSP of Kapurthala, wanted to meet with him. When Jagvinder did not return home, his parents contacted the bar associations in Jullandhar, where Jagvinder practiced, and in Kapurthala, where he had formerly practiced. The bar associations met with SSP Tiwari, but he denied any knowledge of Jagvinder's detention. The delegations then met with the Chief Minister who appointed the DIG from Jullandhar to conduct an investigation. The DIG also denied that Jagvinder was in the custody of either the Kapurthala or the Jullandhar police. After lawyers from both bar associations picketed the house of the SSP on October 30, 1992, Chief Minister Beant Singh appointed a committee of two ministers to inquire into the incident and report back in a week. As of April 1994, the committee had not given its report.

Disappearances in Jeobala

V. Singh, aged thirty-five, a resident of the village of Jeobala in Amritsar district, told HRW/PHR that on July 23, 1992, at about 9:00 P.M. the police surrounded his house. They asked for a relative of V.'s, Piara Singh, by name, and, when he answered, the police hit him with rifle butts on his face. They then ordered Piara, aged sixty, his cousin V., Piara's son H. Singh, aged twenty-two, V.'s nephew Gurdeep Singh, aged twenty-five, and Swaran Singh, the father-in-law of Piara's daughter, outside and tied their hands behind their backs and ordered V. to drive them on his tractor up to the road where the police jeeps and vans were parked. Everyone but V. was ordered to get into a police van; V. was ordered to drive back to his house. The police then drove off with the four other men but did not tell V. where they were being taken.

V. later heard from a released detainee that he had seen the four at the Goindwal police station on the night of July 23. When V. went to the police station at 10:00 A.M. on July 25, he recognized one of the officers who had come to his house: Sawinderpal Singh. When V. confronted him, Sawinderpal Singh told him: "This time you have said it was me but if you say it again, then we will also bury you in here." Afraid he might also be detained, V. left.

On July 31 Gurdeep Singh managed to get a note to V. to tell him that he and Swaran were at the Verowal police station. However, when V. went there, the police did not allow him in.

On August 11, one of V.'s co-workers at the Punjab State Electricity Board saw Gurdeep and Piara sitting in a police van in Jhabal township. When he stopped and asked permission to talk to them, the constable told him that he could talk to them until his superior returned. Gurdeep told the co-worker that he and Piara had been detained in the Jhabal police station for the previous three days and that they were supposed to be questioned by the army that day and then released. The co-worker told V. that Gurdeep appeared to be in pain and had difficulty climbing back into van.

When the two men were not released, V. met with the SSP, Ajit Singh, who told him to bring the co-worker who saw Piara and Gurdeep in the van. When the co-worker came and repeated to the SSP what he had seen, the SSP accused him of collecting false witnesses. V. then made inquiries from army officials posted in the area and was told that the men would be released on August 11 or 12. However, the next day the battalion was transferred to Ludhiana. V. went to Ludhiana but was told that the colonel he had spoken to was on leave.

Gurdeep's employer, the Punjab State Electricity Board, also petitioned the police for information about Gurdeep but never received any information.

Hardeep Singh

On June 7, 1992, Hardeep Singh, aged eighteen, a resident of Mohalli, disappeared after being taken into custody by the Punjab police.[44] According to relatives, about fifty uniformed policemen from the Mohalli police station arrived at Hardeep's house at about 11:00 P.M. They were led by SHO Purshottam Singh. When the police saw Hardeep

---

[44] In May 1992, Hardeep was briefly detained following a dispute with a neighbor at their family home in Mallaya, Jandiala, district Amritsar.

III. Human Rights Violations by Government Forces   47

inside the house, they asked his name and as soon as Hardeep told them, they removed his turban and used it to tie his hands behind his back and took him away. They told his family that they were taking him for investigation because another suspect in a case had named him. He was never produced in court.

On June 9, his relatives sent a petition asking for information about Hardeep to the SP for Ropar district, Senior Superintendent (SSP) Sajjin Gupta and the Inspector General (Vigilance), Mohinder Singh. On June 16 they sent a petition to the Governor. The next day, as they were making inquiries the deputy superintendent of police (DSP) in Mohalli told them that Hardeep had been transferred to the CIA staff headquarters in Ropar. On June 18, DSP Chahal told them that Hardeep would be released in eight days. But when the family returned on that day, the DSP told them that he had been informed the day before that Hardeep would not be released. On June 22, the family met again with SSP Sajjin Gupta and IG Mohinder Singh, but both of them denied that Hardeep was in custody.

Through August 20, the family continued to meet with Purshottam Singh, the SHO who had taken Hardeep into custody. During these meetings, he promised that he would ask Inspector Jaspal Singh to look into the matter and let them know.

The factory owner for whom Hardeep worked, A. Singh, was arrested two days before Hardeep along with two others and was detained for twenty-three days. A. Singh told the family that he had been with Hardeep for fourteen days at the CIA staff headquarters in Ropar. He said that when he saw him, Hardeep told him he had been tortured with electric shock and by having his legs stretched. He was in pain and was unable to move without great difficulty.

In October 1992, we met with the local member of the state legislative assembly (MLA), who stated that after receiving complaints about the case, he had contacted another SSP, Swaran Singh, who agreed to meet with him alone. The meeting took place around September 30. The MLA recounted the conversation he had with the SSP:

> The SSP told me Hardeep had run away. I said, "How could he run when he could not even move?" Then SSP said, "You are intelligent, you should understand." I said, "Is he no more?" The SSP again said, "You are intelligent, you understand everything, why do you ask

us?" Since then I have received an anonymous letter, in Punjabi, saying that the writer was in police custody with Hardeep, and that he saw the police carry out his body one day. The case has been marked for magisterial inquiry but it has not begun. When I saw the subdivisional magistrate about it he said, "Since Hardeep is no more, why do you press for inquiry?"

Paramjit Singh

On June 1, 1992, at about 4:00 A.M., some ten to fifteen Punjab police jeeps from the CIA staff headquarters in Chandigarh surrounded the home of Paramjit Singh[45] in Chandigarh. Some of the police took positions on the courtyard walls surrounding the house; others entered the house and questioned Paramjit's father, G. Singh. They asked him whether Gurcharan Singh Tohra, an Akali Dal leader, had come to the house. Paramjit's father told the police that Tohra had never been there, and explained that there may have been some confusion because his own name was similar. The police then asked for Paramjit and began searching the house. When they found Paramjit and a friend who had spent the night sleeping on the roof,[46] the police beat the two men. They tied their hands behind their backs with their turbans and forced them into two police vans. Then they started beating other members of the family and pushed each of them into a police van: G., his elder son, Mo., his wife, Ba. Kaur, their infant, and another son, Ma. All of the

---

[45] Paramjit was previously arrested on June 24, 1987, when he had gone to the Golden Temple for a meeting of the All-India Sikh Students Federation, a political group whose members generally subscribe to a strict interpretation of Sikh practices and whose leaders have sometimes aligned themselves with militant demands. He was jailed until 1990.

[46] In the hot season, when temperatures reach 120 degrees, it is common for people in Punjab to sleep on the roof or in the courtyard.

III. Human Rights Violations by Government Forces   49

detainees were taken to CIA staff headquarters in Chandigarh, Sector 11. By this time it was about 5:00 A.M.[47]

When they reached the CIA staff headquarters, Paramjit and his friend were taken to one room. The rest of the family could hear their cries until about 10:00 A.M. when they saw them being taken out into the courtyard of the police station. Both men were naked and were placed in the sun where it was very hot. One of the policemen came over to Paramjit holding a black cord that was attached to a transformer box. He appeared to administer shocks to Paramjit, who began to shake. This went on for about forty-five minutes. Sometimes when Paramjit appeared to faint, one of the police would throw water on him from bucket. After that, the police picked up Paramjit and took him away.

Then G., Mo. and Ma. were brought out into the courtyard.

> We were made to sit in the sun, and as the police walked by they gave each of us a slap or a punch. From where we were sitting we could see Paramjit with his hands tied behind his back and a rope tied under his arms around his chest that was attached to a hook on the ceiling. He was hanging with his feet three feet off the ground. He was surrounded by about ten policemen, some in uniform, the rest in civil dress. Two of them were beating him on the soles and tops of his feet with lathis and small batons. When he passed out, they threw water on him, then resumed the beating. He was naked.

After about an hour, Paramjit was taken down and G. and his two sons were taken to see the SHO of the Sector 11 police station and SSP

---

[47] After arresting the five family members on June 1, the police locked the house and took the keys. The keys were not returned to Paramjit's mother, Pritam Kaur, despite repeated requests, until August 19, although she was once permitted to go into the house to get some clothes. When the keys were finally returned, the family discovered that Rs. 4,000 [$133] were missing, along with some gold ornaments, telephone equipment, a scooter, and some pens and calculators from the shop attached to the house.

Saini.[48] Paramjit was not there. Saini ordered G. and Ba. Kaur shifted to the Sector 11 police station. When they came out of the room, they saw Paramjit sitting on the veranda in front of the courtyard. He was naked and bleeding.

At 4:00 P.M., G. and Ba. were taken to the Sector 11 police station and detained in the lock-up. On the afternoon of June 4, G. and Ba. were taken back to CIA staff headquarters. Then they were taken out and the police pointed out Paramjit to them, saying, "See, he's safe." Paramjit was dressed and conscious, but was standing with difficulty and appeared to have lost weight. They were not allowed to speak to him. One of the inspectors told them that nothing had been found against the rest of the family, except Paramjit, and everyone but him would be sent home. He told them, "Paramjit will take some time, but we will not kill him."

After they were detained, Pr. Kaur, G. Singh's wife, filed a habeas corpus writ petition in the High Court at Chandigarh. On June 22 she saw Paramjit in Nabha prison. He was walking with difficulty and had lost weight. She was permitted to see him only for about five minutes. Although G. and Ma. were in the same prison, Paramjit did not know that they were there and they were not allowed to meet him or each other.

When Pr. came back to see Paramjit again on June 26, she was told that he had been taken on police remand by the Mohalli police. Paramjit was to be produced in court on July 8, but he was not. The family's lawyer filed another application in the High Court asking for Paramjit to be produced. At a hearing on July 10, the judge ordered the police to produce Paramjit by July 17. On that day, the police counsel appeared in court and told the judge that the police had attempted to transfer Paramjit to Ropar, but when they reached the Bhakara canal, the jeep got a flat tire, and Paramjit, who was handcuffed, "jumped into the canal and escaped."

Then G. and Ba. Kaur were taken back to SSP Saini and the SHO of Mohalli. Saini told them he was sending the men to their residence under the guard of the SHO, and that Ba. Kaur would be sent to her parents in Ludhiana. However, the SHO brought them instead to the Mohalli police station where G. and Ma. were both put in the police lock-

---

[48] SSP Saini has been named by victims and family members in numerous cases of torture, disappearances and extrajudicial killings. Despite evidence that he has ordered or otherwise participated in these abuses, to HRW's knowledge, no action has ever been taken against him. See also Asia Watch, *Punjab in Crisis*.

III. Human Rights Violations by Government Forces

up, and Ba. was sent to a room on the first floor. The police told Ba. that they were taking Mo. to his job at a power plant in Ropar; the family later learned that Mo. was sent to the CIA staff headquarters in Ropar. The next day, Ba. was taken to her parents house.

On June 7, G. and Ma. were produced before a magistrate at Kharar. The magistrate ordered them to be placed in judicial custody in Ropar prison, but instead, the police took them back to the Mohalli lock-up and the next day they were taken to Nabha prison and charged with harboring a terrorist. The police report claimed they were arrested on June 6.[49] The men were granted bail on July 29, but because they feared that if they accepted it, they would be implicated in other cases, they remained in jail. On August 31, Pr. Kaur spoke with SP Jagdish Kumar of Mohalli who told her that the men were not needed. She paid the surety of Rs. 15,000 [$500], and the men were released.

The police record on Mo. claimed that he was arrested from his residence in Ropar on June 6, produced before the magistrate on June 7, and then remanded to judicial custody. He was also charged with harboring a terrorist. He was bailed out on June 13 after providing a surety of Rs. 5,000 [$166].

Param Satinderjit Singh

Param Satinderjit Singh, a student at Guru Nanak Dev University in Amritsar, was detained by the police on May 18, 1992. G., a fellow student, told us that at about 5:30 P.M. that day, Param was in a sweet shop on Lawrence Road in Amritsar when about seven policemen arrested him. The next day, Dr. Atamjit Singh, the dean of student welfare, went to the police but was told that Param was not in custody. After the students launched a hunger strike on September 9, the dean of students, Dr. Kashmir Singh, the president of the teachers union, Dr. Ghumman, and two student leaders, including G., met with the SSP of Amritsar, Hardeep Singh Dhillon. The SSP told them that Param had been detained, but not by his police but by police belonging to some other district who were operating in the area without permission. When the delegation asked how this was possible, he told them:

---

[49] Under Indian law, a detainee must be produced before a magistrate within twenty-four hours of arrest. In Punjab and elsewhere police routinely falsify arrest records to circumvent the law.

You cannot always talk in legal terms; the law only exists in the books. There was a 99 percent chance that the boy has been killed.

On September 23, a delegation of Dr. Atamjit Singh, Dr. Kawaljit Singh, the head of the physical education department, and two students, including G., met with the Chief Secretary, a state government official, A.S. Chatha. Chatha told them several times that he had information that Param was still in custody and he would be found in a couple of days. He also told them that Param was a terrorist and that he had been involved in a bombing incident, but that the police had not registered a case against him because they could find no witnesses. Chatha also told them he would make sure that Param was not tortured and that he would be sent to judicial custody under TADA or the NSA, and that his parents and the dean of students welfare would be permitted to see him within a few days. However, they were not permitted to see Param and the police provided no further information about Param.

Param's father told us that he had been told that Param was wanted by the Gurdaspur police, and that the police who detained him were from the Dhariwal police station in Gurdaspur district.

Amarjit Singh

On May 17, 1992, at about 2:00 P.M. police from the Bareta police station surrounded the house of Amarjit Singh, aged nineteen, in the village of Balran, in district Sangrur. Amarjit, who was ill with dysentery, was resting at home. According to family members who witnessed the arrest, the police entered the house without warning and hit Amarjit with their rifle butts. They then forced him get into the police van and drove off. According to local residents, after the van reached the village center, the police tied Amarjit's hands behind his back and blindfolded him. When the family inquired at the police station about Amarjit's whereabouts, the Bareta police denied arresting him; he has never been produced in court.

Amarjit's older brother, Malkiat, who had allegedly joined a militant group, was reported killed in an "encounter" on May 30.

Harjinder Singh

III. Human Rights Violations by Government Forces 53

On May 15 or 16, 1992, police from the CIA staff headquarters in Ludhiana raided the house of P. Singh, aged twenty-eight, a farmer and resident of Dakha village, in Ludhiana district. When they could not find P. Singh at home, they arrested his younger brother Pr. Singh and a friend, Harjinder Singh. Pr.'s hands were tied behind his back and he was taken to CIA staff headquarters. After the family and the village sarpanch promised to produce P. Singh, Pr. was released the next day. However, Harjinder was not released. A few days after he was detained, a police report was published in the local newspaper claiming that a militant, Harjinder of village Talwandi, committed suicide after being surrounded by the police. The police never acknowledged that Harjinder was in custody.[50]

Gulab Singh

On May 1, 1992, at about 3:30 P.M. the Punjab police arrested Gulab Singh from his residence in the village of Bakhora Kalam. The police told the family that he was wanted by Subinspector Gulzar Singh of the Moomak police station, who was known to the family. R. Singh, a neighbor, accompanied Gulab Singh as far as the police van, which was parked on the outskirts of the village. R. said the police did not look familiar, but Gulab got in the van anyway and the police drove off.

After they left, R., accompanied by an acquaintance who was a prominent union leader in the area, went to the Moomak police station to inquire about Gulab. They were told that Gulab was not in custody. The next day R. went to the deputy inspector general (DIG) in Patiala, who told him to see the SSP, but because the SSP was not available he met the superintendent of operations, who told him that he would inquire and that R. should come back the next day. When he returned the next day, however, R. was detained. The police accused him of providing shelter to militants and ordered him to tell them the whereabouts of G.'s brother, who was alleged to have joined a militant group. R. denied knowing anything, and the police threatened to torture him with the roller, but they released him after eight days. Afterwards, R. continued to

---

[50] P. was later brought to the police station by the panchayat and questioned about a militant leader. He was detained again later and tortured. For more on the case, see p.71.

meet with police officials about G. but learned nothing. The police only pressed him to help them arrest G.'s brother.

G.'s older brother, S., aged sixty, was also detained, on August 4, 1992. He was taken at 1:30 A.M. to Moonak police station, and held until September 23, 1992. He was not tortured. He was also told to produce the other brother.

M. Singh and son U. Singh

A. Kaur, aged forty-five, told PHR/HRW that on November 16, 1991 she witnessed the arrest of her husband, M. Singh, aged fifty-four, and son, U. Singh, aged twenty-three, both taxi drivers. At about 7:30 A.M. that day, approximately fifteen police from the Sector 39 police station, led by SHO Om Prakash and ASI Kishen Lar, surrounded their house. A. stated:

> My husband and son had never had any problems with the police. The police came and took them away without telling me or my daughter anything. I immediately contacted the SSP of Chandigarh who told me that my son and husband would be in custody for one week and then they would be released. They would not let me see them. After a week, I contacted the SSP again. This time, he told me, "They have been transferred elsewhere and we haven't seen them since." I contacted the SHO and inspector at the Sector 9 police station and SSP Saini. All of them denied knowing the whereabouts of my husband and son. On December 10, 1991, a man by the name of G. Singh came to my home and told me that on November 19, he and my husband were both held in the Sector 3 police station and kept in the same cell for several days. G. Singh said that my husband was so badly tortured that he was unable to walk. G. Singh was released after that; he never saw my son.

B. Kaur, aged twenty-four, the daughter of A. Kaur, corroborated the above testimony of the arrest of her father and brother as well as the information provided by G. Swaran. The family has been unable to discover the whereabouts and condition of M. and U.

III. Human Rights Violations by Government Forces

L. Singh

L. Singh had worked undercover as a "black cat" agent for the police in Majitha since October 1989. On February 12, 1991, at about midnight, his brother-in-law, B., took L.'s AK-47 rifle, 250 cartridges, two grenades, one bolt-action rifle, and fled. When L. discovered the missing weapons, he attempted to track down B. in his home village, but learned that B. had picked up his wife early in the morning and left the village. L. then informed Inspector Sukhvinder Singh of the CIA staff in Majitha of what had happened. After searching L.'s house, L. was detained at the police station.

On February 16, L. was dismissed from the police, and he was charged with conspiracy under Section 380/409/120B of the Indian Penal Code. L. was permitted visits by family members until February 27. On that day they were told that they could not see him. DSP Gurmeet Singh told them, "For what purpose have you brought tea when he is no longer here? He has already been shifted to the Beas police station."

At Beas the family was told by SHO Rajinder Singh, DSP Baba Bakala and Officer Darshan Singh that L. was not there. The next day the SHO and DSP again denied that L. was there. On February 28, SSP Paramjit Singh Gill told the family that L. had been "sent on an operation." DIG Bhullar denied knowing anything about L.'s whereabouts.

The family filed a writ of habeas corpus on March 16, 1991. Since then, there has been a judicial inquiry to establish the facts of the case. SSP Paramjit Singh Gill appeared for the defense and denied any wrong doing by the police. The whereabouts of L. remain unknown.

Torture

International human rights law prohibits torture and other cruel, inhuman or degrading treatment or punishment. The International Covenant on Civil and Political Rights (ICCPR), the Convention against Torture and Other Cruel, Inhuman or Degrading Treatment, and the

Code of Conduct for Law Enforcement Officers all explicitly ban torture.[51] India has yet to ratify the Convention Against Torture, and is among more than seventy countries that practice torture systematically.[52]

Torture is widely used in Punjab as a means of coercing detainees to provide information or to confess, punishing persons believed sympathetic to the militants and creating a climate of political repression. Although perpetrators attempt to justify torture on the basis of gaining

---

[51] The Convention against Torture and Other Cruel, Inhuman or Degrading Treatment or Punishment defines torture, in Article 1, as "any act by which severe pain or suffering, whether physical or mental is intentionally inflicted on a person for such purposes as obtaining from him or a third person information or a confession, punishing him for an act he or a third person has committed or is suspected of having committed, or intimidating or coercing him or a third person, or for any reason based on discrimination of any kind, when such pain and suffering is inflicted by or at the instigation of or with the consent or acquiescence of a public official." Article 2 states that "no exceptional circumstances whatsoever, whether . . . internal political stability or any other public emergency may be invoked as a justification of torture." Article 4 states that "each State Party shall ensure that all acts of torture are offenses under its criminal law. The same shall apply to an attempt to commit torture and to an act by any person which constitutes complicity or participation in torture."

[52] Torture is widely used by Indian police and other security forces, not only in areas of insurgency but throughout the country. It is used not only against political detainees, but also against petty criminals and persons who have committed no crime at all. Those most vulnerable are the poor, members of "scheduled" castes and tribes, "dalits" (untouchables), landless laborers and women. See Amnesty International, *India: Torture, Rape & Deaths in Custody*, (London: Amnesty International Publications, 1992). For an overview on the worldwide practice of torture see *Amnesty International Report 1992* (London: Amnesty International Publications, 1992) and M. Basoglu, *Torture and its Consequences: Current Treatment Approaches* (New York: Cambridge University Press, 1992, pp. 82-106). The general practice of torture among police and paramilitary forces throughout India may, in fact, account for its routine use in India's disturbed areas; regarding torture in Punjab, see Asia Watch, *Punjab in Crisis: Human Rights in India* (New York: Human Rights Watch, 1991) and for Kashmir, see *The Human Rights Crisis in Kashmir: A Pattern of Impunity* (New York and Boston: Human Rights Watch and Physicians for Human Rights, 1993) and Asia Watch, *Kashmir Under Siege* (May 1991).

III. Human Rights Violations by Government Forces

information and of meting out punishment, the fundamental purpose of torture appears to be to inflict severe physical and psychological pain in order to destroy the dignity and will of individuals and to repress potential support for political opponents by indiscriminately targeting members of certain political groups or social communities.

Torture is facilitated by the fact that security personnel routinely ignore procedural safeguards when taking persons into custody. Although Indian law requires that everyone taken into custody must be produced before a magistrate within twenty-four hours, in fact, detainees are rarely produced at all.[53] Prohibitions and safeguards against torture in the Indian Penal Code (IPC) and the Code of Criminal Procedure (CCrP),[54] which prohibit the use of coerced confessions and prescribe inquiries into deaths in custody and prison terms for officers guilty of torture, are also routinely disregarded. Detainees are frequently held in incommunicado detention, which also increases the risk of torture. To our knowledge, security personnel responsible for torture in Punjab have never been held criminally liable for their actions.[55] A police officer interviewed on condition of anonymity told us:

> In my training as a police officer, I learned that torture was prohibited by Indian law. However, "third degree" interrogation, which may involve beating, is not generally considered torture. Once I became a police officer in Punjab, I realized that torture is used routinely.

---

[53] Under Article 9 of the ICCPR, "Anyone arrested or detained on a criminal charge shall be brought promptly before a judge or other officer authorized by law. . . and shall be entitled to a trial within a reasonable time or released."

[54] Sections 330 and 331 of the Indian Penal Code prescribe prison terms and fines for officers guilty of torture. Section 176 of the CCrP requires a magisterial inquiry into any death in custody. The Indian Evidence Act and the CCrP also prohibit the use of coerced confessions.

[55] Government officials claim that they have punished security personnel for abuses in Punjab, but they have never made public the nature of the abuses, the identity and rank of those responsible for abuses, and what punishments have been ordered.

> During my give years with the Punjab police, I estimate 4,000 to 5,000 were torture at my police station alone.

Another retired police officer told us:

> The Punjab Police Rules emphasize that minimum force should be used in questioning suspects. Before 1980, the "third degree" was not used very much and was much less than what it is now. It used to involve beating. This was usually done with lathis or a leather belt. In the British time, the leather belt was the sole of a shoe. In the early 1970s, I recall the SP from Ropar killed someone by a "fake encounter." He is now DGP. There were some custodial deaths at that time. Several died in custody, but they were not revealed. About 1976, Sradjit Singh, the SSP of Ludhiana, now DIG, introduced electric shock to the police station. The roller method of torture started prior to 1980; suspension, after 1980; and leg stretching more recently. Torturers are selected on the basis of their mind setting: For example, one who shows a tendency. If he does not comply, he will be suspended or dismissed. Mostly, they do it drunk. Then, after they get accustomed to it, they do it sober. There is no extra pay, but he expects favors, like an out-of-turn promotion. An SI may become DSP in just a few months for torturing. The procedure for internal police investigation is at the level of SSP. In some cases there may be a special investigative board from district head-quarters or from another police station. The most severe form of discipline would be dismissals and prosecution, but this is very rare. When action is taken, it is usually departmental discipline.

Police also arrest and torture detainees for the purpose of extorting bribes. According to this retired police officer, "the distribution of bribe money these days depends on the people involved, but generally the DSP and above get 'big money,' 25 to 50 percent of their salary."

Torture in Punjab is practiced in police stations, and in staff headquarters of the CIA located in district centers and other larger towns.

III. Human Rights Violations by Government Forces

Special interrogation centers, such as that at Mal Mandi in Taran Taran, have become notorious for torture. Police have also tortured detainees in private facilities outside of regular police and security buildings. We interviewed police who testified that they routinely tortured suspected militants and anyone who has contact with militants, under orders of their superiors and with the knowledge of the central government. Considering that tens of thousands of persons have been detained under anti-terrorism legislation between 1982 and 1994, conservative estimates of the number tortured would clearly be at least in the thousands.

Our findings are based on first-hand testimony by torture victims. When possible, physical examinations were conducted to evaluate physical evidence of torture. In the first five cases described below, the examinations were conducted in the United States, and the victims were asylum applicants who had fled India.

Methods of torture include electric shock, prolonged beatings with canes and leather straps, tying the victim's hands and suspending him or her from the ceiling, pulling the victim's legs far apart so as to cause great pain, and rotating a heavy wooden or metal roller over the thighs. Psychological forms of torture often include death threats, disrobing, isolation, and forcing family members to watch as a relative is tortured.

As one police officer noted:

> Without exception, any person who is detained at the police station is tortured. The methods of torture range from beatings with a leather strap or wooden club, to suspension from the ceiling, to use of a heavy wooden roller which is moved up and down a detainee's thighs to the stretching apart of the detainee's legs at the crotch. The torture is intended to elicit information regarding the names of militants, whereabouts of weapons caches or information regarding future plans of the militants. Those who were suspected of being militants, but gave no information during torture, are tortured to death. Anyone who admitted to being a militant or of supporting militants is also killed. Also, the torture is intended to punish those whom the police authorities and government suspect of harboring pro-Khalistan sympathies. For example, those who are suspected of providing shelter to militants are routinely detained and

tortured to send a message to all Sikhs not to support the militants or the movement for Khalistan in any way. If the torture victim is too brutally tortured or if serious injury results from the torture, the detainee is executed in a false "encounter."

B. Singh

B. Singh, 23, a farmer from Akalpur village in the district of Jalandhar, told PHR/HRW about his detention and torture in December 1993:

> When the police first came to our house in 1991, they accused us of sheltering terrorists and storing weapons. Militants did use a path near our property, but we never had any contact with them. The police searched our home and the pump house and found nothing. We told them that we had not helped anyone. One of them noticed the tattoo on my hand, which says "Ek-omkar." This means "one god" in Punjabi. Several of my friends and I had it done at a religious fair in 1990. The police demanded to know why I had the tattoo and said I was trying to prove that I was the "greatest Sikh" by displaying the tattoo. They threatened to take me to the police station and make a "martyr" of me. After this, the police visited our house every few months and continued to harass and threaten us.

In early December 1993, five men were killed by police in the nearby village of Kanga. About three weeks later, B. was arrested at his home by Punjab Police and CRPF soldiers and taken with six other young men from his village to Pillhaur Police Station. B. was taken to a cell with the others: A. Singh[56], Phuwinder Singh, Gurnam Singh, Amar Singh, Narinder Singh and Jaswant Singh. He recounted:

> One by one, we were taken to another room. I could hear the screams of my friends before it was my turn. I

---

[56]See testimony of A. Singh on p.61 .

III. Human Rights Violations by Government Forces

> was the third one to be tortured. There were about five police in the room. One of them said: "If you tell us where you have hidden the weapons, we will release you." I told them I knew nothing about weapons. They began slapping and punching me. They forced me to lie on the ground and with wooden rods they beat the soles of my feet until I nearly lost consciousness. I was then made to stand on my feet while they repeatedly struck my thighs and calves with the wooden rods. I lost consciousness, but awoke soon after when water was thrown on my face and I was pulled to my feet by my hair. They beat the soles of my feet again before I was returned to the cell.

B. and the others were released the following day after the sarpanch and about twenty-five others from his village petitioned for their release. After his release, B. remained in hiding for approximately one month before leaving India to seek asylum in the United States. He was interviewed and examined in March 1994. When PHR's Dr. Iacopino examined B., he had recovered physically from the abuse he described and had no specific findings on physical examination as is often the case following blunt trauma.

A. Singh

A. Singh, aged twenty-one, a farmer from Akalpur village in the district of Jalandhar, described his experience of torture by police in mid-December 1993. He was arrested and tortured with B. Singh[57] and five other young men from his village. He stated that he was not politically active and had no contact with militants.

> In the morning, while I was feeding our cattle, about six Punjab police and four CRPF came to my house and accused me of providing shelter to militants. I told them I had not. "We'll take you in and make you admit it," one of them said. I was taken to Phillaur police station with six other boys from my village. We were all kept in

---

[57]See testimony of B. Singh on p.60.

a cell and tortured one by one. I was the fourth one. The police accused me, saying: "Militants come to your house. Why do you not tell us?" "Militants had never come to my home," I told them. They began slapping me and forced me to lie on the floor. As two policemen restrained me, several others beat the soles of my feet for about ten minutes. They also struck my shoulders and back with the wooden rods. We were all released the following day.

After A.'s release, he fled India to seek asylum in the U.S. PHR interviewed him in March 1994. When PHR's Dr. Iacopino examined A., he had fully recovered from the abuse he described and had no specific findings on physical examination as is often the case following blunt trauma.

M. Singh

M. Singh, a 46-year-old amritdhari Sikh farmer from the district of Ludhiana, was first arrested, along with his family, in August 1990. He was accused of supporting the militants after some militants came to his house and forced M. to provide them with food and shelter. The police beat M. and threatened to kill his family. His wife told him that the police had kissed and fondled her. The police released M. and his wife after the village sarpanch intervened and a Rs. 30,000 [$1,000] bribe was paid. A few weeks later, M. was again arrested and tortured with severe beatings and by having his legs stretched apart until he fainted. M. and his wife were released the next day with the help of the village panchayat and family members who paid Rs. 23,000 [$ 767] for their release. After that incident, the family moved to the neighboring state of Rajasthan. M. described how he was arrested again in November 1993 and tortured:

> In mid-November 1993, a raiding party of about fifteen CRPF and Rajasthan police arrested me. The police told me that I "could not escape" and asked, "so why have you fled Punjab?" They took me to Bharatpur police station in Delhi. During the night, policemen slapped and kicked me and whipped me with a leather strap. The next morning, I was taken to the police station in

III. Human Rights Violations by Government Forces

> Ludhiana and turned over to the Punjab police. Over the next two days, I was severely beaten with fists, wooden rods and leather straps. My wife got word to a relative and they secured my release with a bribe. Before letting me go, the police warned me that it was the last time they were releasing me.

Soon after M. was reunited with his family, they fled India.

S. Singh

S. Singh, aged twenty-eight, a barber from Dalle Wallah village in the district of Jalandhar, described how he was tortured in 1991 and again in 1993.

> For as many generations as I can remember, all the men in my family have been barbers. I began cutting hair in 1989. About one year later, two men from my village, Satpal Dhillon and Harminder Singh, told me to close our shop as cutting hair was against the Sikh religion. My brother P. and I closed our shop, but periodically reopened to enable us to support our family. Once when we had opened the shop, the police came and threatened to arrest us if we did not keep the shop opened. In the later part of 1991, the police came to my house and accused us of closing our shop out of sympathy for the militants. We were taken to Goraya police station and placed in a cell. I was taken out to the verandah first. There where about ten policemen present. They made me lie face down and began beating the soles of my feet with wooden rods. Then, they removed my pants and had me lie on my back. A heavy wooden roller was then placed on my thighs and moved back and forth. Several policemen also repeatedly forced my legs apart as far as they could go. Two policemen had to help me back to the cell because I could not walk. Then, they took my brother out to the verandah where I could hear him screaming. We were released on the following day through the help of the village sarpanch and panchayat.

Towards the end of 1992, my uncle and I were arrested by police who were looking for a man named G. I had a brother by the same name, but he had not lived in Punjab for more than ten years. The police then picked up another man in our village with the same name as by brother G. and we were all taken to Goraya police station. G. was taken out of the cell first and returned about an hour later, unable to speak or walk. My uncle was then interrogated about my brother G. About five hours later, my uncle and I were released with the help of the panchayat. In mid-1993, I was again arrested by police. They said they had warned me before and I had still not opened my barber shop. I was taken to Goraya police station and after about five hours was taken to the verandah and beaten. They used wooden rods and beat me on my arms and legs, chest, back and buttocks. I fell to the ground. The pain was unbearable. I pleaded with them to stop beating me and to just shoot me. They continued to beat me for about 25 minutes. When they were finished, one of them said: "If you don't listen, we will torture you again and kill you. "

After S.'s release, he fled India to seek asylum in the United States, where PHR interviewed and examined him in March 1994. The examination revealed several linear scars on his chest and back consistent with laceration injuries.

A. Singh

A. Singh, 39, an amritdhari Sikh farmer from Nurpur Hakima village, in district Ferozpur, told PHR/HRW about repeated arrests and torture by police between 1984 and 1993. He was suspended and beaten on the shins, his legs were repeatedly pulled apart, and he was subjected to the roller treatment. He was also given electric shock and repeatedly kicked in the testicles. Once, when A. was struck with a wooden rod to the right chest, a blood clot developed under his skin and he was taken to Mallanwala police station where a doctor surgically removed it. He was also whipped on his back and buttocks with a leather strap which was painted with the slogan, "come and love me." In 1988, A. went into hiding

III. Human Rights Violations by Government Forces

in the state of Assam. In March 1993, a friend of A. revealed A's. whereabouts under torture by police. A. told PHR:

> SP Rupinder Singh Bajwa and about thirty Punjab police and CRPF came to where I was staying in Assam. While en route to Punjab, we stopped at a forest and I was beaten with rifle butts and wooden rods. They demanded the names of militants who were hiding outside of Punjab. I told them I had fled to save my life and was not involved with any militants. They continued to beat me. I was taken to Sadar police station in Ferozpur and detained for about three weeks. During that time, I was tortured two to three times a day under the direct supervision of SP Rupinder Singh, SHO Avtar Singh and DSP Dhawan. They demanded to know the whereabouts of militants and weapons. I was stripped naked and beaten many times. My legs were stretched apart and the iron roller was used on my legs. A wooden rod was placed behind my knees and my legs were pressed towards my buttocks. They brought in a young man who was badly tortured. "He has agreed to tell us about the militants," they said. "If you do not disclose anything, you will be shot and your body thrown into the canal." One night the they blindfolded me and took me outside of the police station. I was made to stand in front of a tree. They told me: "Help us or we will kill you." I said I had nothing to tell them. I thought for sure they were going to kill me. They fired their guns close to my head and intentionally missed. Then, we returned to the police station.

A. was then produced before a magistrate in Ferozpur and charged with illegal possession of firearms. After two months in Ferozpur Central Jail, he was released on bail. Soon after, A. fled India. Police have continued to visit A's. home, and have detained his father as recently as February, 1994. When PHR's Dr. Iacopino examined A. in March 1994, he had striking physical evidence of the abuse he described. There were areas of marked atrophy (tissue loss) and fibrosis (scaring) of both left and right anterior thigh muscles, consistent with extensive muscle damage from the roller method of torture. There was a twelve-centimeter surgical scar present in the right lateral chest wall where a large hematoma was said to have been removed and a two-centimeter surgical scar in the left groin area. There was a bony deformity and callus formation present over the left shin, indicating a possible old fracture where the roller had been applied.

H. Singh

H. Singh, aged fifty-one, an electrician and resident of the village of Dakha Village, told us about the killing of his son Navtej, aged twenty-five, in October 1992.[58] Several months before the killing, in April 1992, H. was picked up by police from the Sadar police station in Ludhiana who were looking for Navtej.[59]

H. told HRW/PHR:

> For the first twenty-four hours, I was not given any food or water. After four days, I told the police that if they released me, I could bring Navtej to them. The police shouted obscenities, punched and kicked me and threw me to the ground. Then they beat me on the back with a wooden rod. Since then, I have had chronic pain in my back and numbness in my right leg. After that Navtej came to the police station and I was released.

When PHR examined H. in October 1992, he showed the signs of vertebral nerve compression, associated with vertebral disk disease, consistent with the injuries to his back he sustained in custody.

---

[58] Navtej had been detained on two other occasions before he was killed, once in 1990 and again in April 1992. In both cases, his father was picked up prior to Navtej's detention in order to force Navtej to come in to the police station for questioning.

[59] For more on the killing of Navtej, see p.34, 35.

III. Human Rights Violations by Government Forces

S. Singh and Others

S. Singh G., aged forty-seven, told HRW/PHR that on October 4, 1992, Punjab police and BSF, CRPF troops came to Dakha Village about 4:30 A.M. S. told us that he saw Sukhinder and Navtej in custody.[60]

> About fifteen police came to my house looking for J.. My son was staying at another village for recitation of the Holy Book. When I refused to go with them and explained that I had to perform religious rights at the gurdwara, one of them took out a revolver and said, "Either you come or we will shoot, and keep quiet." They took me to Dakha police station and put me in a cell with six others. I recognized four who were from my village: Charan Singh, "Puppy," son of Labh Singh, "Kaka" Singh, son of Ravail Singh, and Gurjit Singh.[61] We were all being held for exchange purposes. The two other boys were not from our village. Our cell was at the corner of the courtyard, adjacent to the latrine. On October 4, on my way to the latrine, I saw Navtej, Sukhminder and Yadinder in the courtyard. They were all in bad shape. Yawinder had just been beaten and needed help to walk. Navtej and Sukhminder were lying on the ground in pain. On the same day, I saw Kamal Singh in the courtyard. After returning from the latrine to my cell I heard him screaming for about fifteen

---

[60] S. was first detained in February of 1990 by police from the Sadar police station who were looking for his son, J., aged twenty-five, a preacher. Members of the village *panchayat* assisted in the exchange of father and son. After two days J. was charged with conspiracy and possession of a knife, and was remanded to Central Jail, Ludhiana. J. told his father that, while he was detained, he was beaten with leather belts and *lathis* and tortured with leg stretching and the roller. J. was subsequently on bail and acquitted of the first charge. At the time of his arrest in 1992, the second charge was pending a decision which was expected on October 13, 1992. We have not been able to learn the results of the court's decision.

[61] See case of Navtej Singh, p.34, 35.

minutes. On the following day, at about 9:00 A.M., I was taken to another cell. There were about sixteen others in the cell. Among them were Navtej Singh, Yadvinder Singh, Charan Singh, Kamal Singh, Baljinder Singh, "Kaka," son of Ravail Singh and "Puppy," son of Labh Singh. All of them were in severe pain. The boys could hardly move. They kept their legs straight; bending their knees made their pain much worse.

K. Singh

On October 5, 1992, at about 4:30 A.M., the police surrounded the residence of K., aged thirty-four, in the village of Kailay. They asked for K., and when he came out, they asked if anyone was hiding inside the house. K. said that no one was, and the police searched the house. Then they took K. to the Halwara police post, and told him to strip. They tied his hands behind his back with his turban and tortured him by making him lie down while a policeman at either end pulled on his hair and legs and another stomped on his hips and kicked him in the pelvis. When they asked K. if he had served food to militants at his house, he told them he had only done so at gunpoint. Then the police dressed him and took him to the Sudhar police station. The next day at 9:00 A.M. he was taken to see SHO Joginder Singh, who repeated the same accusations and showed K. a file with photographs of militants, and told to identify them but K. told him he could not. The police threatened to beat him again, but did not. K. was released on October 9 at 8:00 A.M.

K. Singh and H. Singh

K. Singh, aged forty-two, from Behla, Taran Taran, told us that on October 4, 1992, he was in the village of Bal Khurd with his cousin D. Singh and D.'s brother, H. At about 4:00 P.M., the house was surrounded by police from the Majitha police station, led by SHO Gurpinder Singh and head constable Sukhdev Singh. When the police learned they were

III. Human Rights Violations by Government Forces

from Behla, K. and H. were detained,[62] while D. was permitted to go to tell their families that they had been arrested.

H. and K. were separated at the police station, and K. was taken to the SHO's office. The SHO accused him of being a militant and told him to "save himself from beatings" by confessing and telling them where he had hidden his weapons. K. told him his name and said that he could check with his employer at the state electricity board for a reference. The SHO then asked him if he was the brother of Sukhdev Singh, to which K. replied that he was not. K. was then ordered to strip, his hands were tied with a rope behind his back and he was hoisted up by the rope and suspended. The police also tied his ankles together and periodically pulled down on his legs. While K. was suspended, the police attached a wire attached to a hand-cranked generator and gave him shocks to his genitals, thighs and chest. After about fifteen minutes of this the SHO said, "Let him cool off and then we will ask again."

K. then saw the police take H. out to the veranda, about ten feet away. They said to him, "[K.] has told us everything (*"bak paya"*); you do the same." Then H. was suspended. After that, the police closed the curtain, and K. could not see him anymore but heard the police ask H. why he was in Behla. H. told them that his wife had had a baby at a nearby hospital in Amritsar on September 24. After about fifteen minutes H. was taken away and K. was again brought out to the veranda. He was stripped, his hands were tied behind his back and he was made to sit on the ground while one policeman pulled his hair and two others pulled his legs out to the side.

> They ordered me to tell them my real name and accused me of being a militant named "Dalla." Finally I told them I was Sukhdev's brother, and they said, "Tell us where the weapons are, or else we will show you killed in an "encounter" [*"Mukabla Bana dena hai"*]."

---

[62] K. was also arrested in 1990 and questioned about his brother after his brother was killed in a police encounter on June 8 or 9, 1992. He was detained at CIA staff headquarters in Taran Taran, and tortured with electric shock to the chest and genitals. He was also suspended and beaten, and had his legs pulled out to the sides. He was held for fifteen days and never produced in court. No case was registered against him. K. was detained five times after that incident, whenever the police were looking for his brother.

After that K. and H. were allowed to get dressed and were fed. H. was released to the panchayat the next day. SHO Gurpinder Singh told K.'s father that he would have to pay RS. 15,000 [$500] or else K. would be sent to Taran Taran.[63] K.'s father promised he would pay Rs. 14,000 [$467]. The money was paid to a friend of the SHO's at 5:00 P.M. on October 8, and at 8:00 P.M. K. was released. No charges were filed against K.

When PHR's Dr. Iacopino examined K. in October 1992, he was still experiencing pain on the insides of his thighs. The physical examination, conducted one day after K.'s release, revealed marked bruising of the muscles of the thighs. The area of bruising on the right side measured 8 x 12 centimeters and 4 x 12 centimeters on the left. These areas were painful to touch, as was any outward movement of the legs.

A. Singh

On September 9, 1992, at about 3:30 A.M., about forty police in four jeeps surrounded the house of A. Singh, aged twenty-eight, in the village of Sarabha and broke open the outer door. A. told us that they grabbed him by his hair and tied his hands behind his back with his turban. They searched the house but took nothing. The police accused him of harboring militants and of acting as a courier for the militants. He was taken to CIA staff headquarters in Ludhiana. There he was taken out to the courtyard and told to strip. He was tortured with the roller, by having his legs stretched, and by being suspended by his hands tied behind his back and beaten. After two days the treatment was repeated and the police also threatened to kill him.

On September 12, when the panchayat came to get him released, a constable was sent to see if he could walk. On finding that A. could not walk, he was not released until September 14 at 8:30 P.M.

After his release, A. was treated in a hospital for continuing pain in his arms and thighs. A. had had no problems with the police before.

Physicians for Human Rights' physical examination of A. in October 1992, revealed a circular scar around the right wrists, consistent with abrasions from rope burns. There was diffuse tenderness of the

---

[63] The Taran Taran police station was notorious for torture.

III. Human Rights Violations by Government Forces

shoulders muscles and a sensory loss in the right forearm suggestive of nerve damage.

P. Singh

On May 15 or 16, 1992, police from the CIA staff headquarters in Ludhiana raided the house of P. Singh, aged twenty-eight, a farmer and resident of Dakha village, in Ludhiana district.[64] When they could not find P. Singh at home, they arrested his younger brother Pr. Singh and a friend Harjinder Singh.[65] When the panchayat brought P. to the CIA staff headquarters, P. was questioned about a militant leader, Kuldip S. Keepa, and the DSP and SP threatened P. that if he did not tell them Keepa's whereabouts he would be killed. P. was released on the condition that he would keep the police informed if he learned anything about Keepa. Fearing that he would be killed, P. left Punjab on June 18 and went to work in Calcutta. After he left, the police again detained Pr. Singh and tortured him for four days. He was released on the condition that the family produce P. Ten days after Pr. was released, the police detained his father, G. Singh. He was also tortured at the CIA staff headquarters for five days.

Upon learning that his family was being harassed, P. returned home. At about 5:00 A.M. on September 12, 1992, police from CIA staff headquarters in Ludhiana raided the house and, not finding P. at home, the police picked up two of his brothers, J. and R., and took them to CIA staff headquarters. They were both tortured. J. was released after three days. The police promised to release R. if P. was brought to them. At 6:30 P.M. on September 17, P., in the presence of the sarpanch, surrendered to the police at the CIA staff in Ludhiana and R. was released.

On the evening of September 19, the police took P. out to the courtyard. He described what happened:

---

[64] P. had previously been arrested on May 23, 1985. He was beaten and tortured with the roller and produced in court on May 28. Four cases were registered against him, and he was transferred to the Central Jail in Ludhiana. In 1988 he was acquitted in all of the cases.

[65] Harjinder subsequently disappeared. For more on the case, see p. 52, 53.

They ordered me to strip, and then lie face down. The police placed a rod behind my thighs just above the knee and my legs were bent over the rod. Then I was pulled by my hair so my feet touched my head. One policeman pulled my arms straight out in front. I passed out and when I came to, they tied my hands behind my back with my turban, and then tied them to a rope which was attached to a rod on the ceiling and a pulley. I was suspended in the air by the pulley while the police beat me with their lathis on the soles of my feet, my ankles and knees, and punched me in the thighs. After about twenty minutes, my left shoulder became dislocated and I passed out. The police reset my shoulder by slamming me against the wall and took me back to the room. My arm was numb and I was unable to move it. When I asked them why they were beating me, they said they had been ordered to by SP Detective B. S. Gill. On September 23 at about 9:30 P.M., SP Detective Gill called me to his room and told me to tell him where Keepa was. He said, "Why are you unnecessarily taking a beating? You should tell." When I told them that I knew nothing, he told the police in the room to beat me. They beat me in his presence. Then they took me to the courtyard and tortured me like they had done before. While they were doing this, the assistant subinspector, Gurchetan Singh, took out a revolver and held it to the side of my head and said that he would shoot unless I told them where Keepa was. Then they took me to SSP Siddhardth Chattopadhya and DSP Detective Shiv Kumar. When I told them I knew nothing about Keepa, SSP Chattopadhyaya said that they would kill me. He said, "Twenty like you die every day, what difference will it make if we kill one more? It's up to you."

Then they took P. back to his room. On September 25, SP Detective B. S. Gill again called P. to his room and asked him why he was not giving them any information. When P. said he did not have any, the SP said, "Either you run away from here or be ready to die." Then he called in a constable, and P. was taken out to a waiting relative and released.

III. Human Rights Violations by Government Forces 73

When PHR's Dr. Iacopino examined P. in October 1992, he was still feeling pain in his side and shoulder and was unable to lift anything. He also had numbness in his forearm. The physical examination revealed damage to the thigh muscles, particularly the right thigh, consistent with the roller method of torture. P. also had a scar indicative of a small laceration to the right forehead and scars on the lower legs and ankles, indicative of abrasion.

Village Gobindpura, in Jawarharwala District

On August 9, 1992, at about 12:30 P.M., a large deployment of the Punjab Police, CRPF, BSF and army surrounded the village of Gobindpura where some members of a militant group had taken refuge. Villagers described an exchange of fire between the militants and the government troops in which one of the militants was killed at about 1:30 P.M. Shortly afterwards, the police used the loudspeaker at the gurdwara to order all the people to assemble at the village school. The security forces ordered sixteen young men to search the houses, using them as civilian shields.[66] One of them, P. Singh, aged twenty-six, described what happened:

> All of us were forced to walk from the school with the security forces behind us. When we reached the center of the village we were divided into four groups of four, with four or five security forces behind. We were told to search each house while they waited outside. We had to let them know if there were any militants inside, or we would be killed. They also said that if we refused or ran away we would be killed. Each group was made to search about fifteen houses.

M. Singh, aged twenty-eight, told us:

> At 6:30 P.M. the firing resumed from one of the houses in which one of the militants were hiding. I hid behind the wall. Then I heard that another one of the militants had been killed. By this time all but two of the sixteen

---

[66] Using civilians as shields is prohibited under international law.

who had been ordered to search the houses were left. Those two were made to search a few more houses until 7:30 P.M.

The security forces kept the place surrounded throughout the next day. The villagers stated that they were kept in the open, even during a heavy rain, and were not provided food or water. Additional security forces arrived, but at about 9:00 P.M. on August 10, the third militant escaped from the village.

The next day at 8:00 A.M., the security forces again took thirty-two persons from the village, divided them into groups of four, and with six or seven CRPF behind them, began to search all the houses in the village. The villagers were released at 7:00 P.M. when the security forces told them, "You are not the ones we want." Over the next several days, they detained a number of people from the village for questioning, including P. Singh, aged twenty-five. He described what happened to him:

> On August 14, at 10:00 A.M. eight policemen came to the gurdwara. First they searched the gurdwara, then they ordered me to come with them to the Lehra police post. I was there for two days, then on the third day I was taken to a room. They removed my clothes and then they accused me of giving shelter to militants. They tied my hands behind my back with rope and suspended me in the air by my hands. They beat me on the soles of my feet, my buttocks and my thighs with a wooden baton and a leather strap. When I fainted, they took me down. When I revived, there were two policemen standing behind me. One of them had his knee in my back and the other was pulling on my hair. At the same time, two policemen on either side pulled apart my legs. This went on for an hour. When I passed out, they would start again after I woke up. Then they tied the big toes of both feet together and made me sit with my legs straight out. They put the roller on my legs, with four policemen standing on it. They did this several times over the next three days. On the fourth day they also beat me with lathis on my ankles, knees, fingers and hands and elbows. The bone of the little finger of my left hand was

dislocated. Two days later, they released me to a relative who paid the surety.

When PHR's Dr. Iacopino examined P. in October 1992, P. complained of chronic pain, weakness and numbness of the left upper shoulder. The physical examination revealed a pattern of muscle weakness and numbness suggestive of nerve damage to the left shoulder and left side of the chest. P. also had distinct circular scars around his wrists, consistent with recent abrasions from rope burns that may have been caused by his being suspended from the wrists.

D. Singh

On June 16 or 17, 1992, D. Singh, an employee at a State Bank in Sangrur, was picked up by the police after a bank robbery at another bank in town.[67] The police first detained his sister-in-law and her children, saying they would only release them if D. turned himself in. The village panchayat met with the police and promised to produce D. if the police would agree to release the family. The relatives were released the next day, and D. was jailed at the Sunam police station. His feet were put in wooden stocks until 11:00 P.M. He told us:

> Then the police made me stand up and they punched me in the face and hit me with their rifle butts and kicked me. One policeman hit me right above the eye with his rifle butt. When I started bleeding they stopped and brought me back to the stocks. In the morning I asked if I could notify my boss, so they let me telephone him and he came down to the jail and told them to release me, as I had been at work at the time of the robbery. He provided surety for my release, and promised to produce me whenever required. I was released that day. I got six stitches for the injury above my eye.

---

[67] D.'s brother, Kesar Singh, was arrested in January 1992 and subsequently killed in an "encounter." For more on the case, see p.33.

When PHR examined D. in October 1992, he had a three-centimeter linear scar above his left eye where he said he was struck with a rifle butt.

Shahid Kartar Singh Memorial Hospital

On or about May 9, 1992, two militants came to the Shahid Kartar Singh Sarabha Hospital in Punjab, seeking emergency treatment. According to a doctor who saw them, one of the men appeared to have consumed cyanide. He was given first-aid, but refused to be admitted to the hospital for further treatment. That night, after the two men left, the house of the general secretary of the hospital's trust fund was raided by police from the Jobha police post and the Sudhar police station. When the police found no one home, they came to the hospital, which is nearby, at about 8:00 or 9:00 P.M. They questioned hospital staff about "the poisoning case" and, when they were told that the case had not been admitted, they searched the hospital for half an hour and then left.

On May 14 at about 4:30 P.M., some fifteen police from the police post surrounded the hospital. At that time a doctor, along with a clerk and driver, had gone in an ambulance to collect medicines from Ludhiana. The police stopped the ambulance outside the Jobha police post and ordered the three occupants into the police station. After questioning, the clerk was released, but the doctor and driver and ambulance were taken to the Sudhar police station. Meanwhile, the hospital was searched and at about 6:30 P.M., Dr. R. was taken to the Sudhar police station. The police questioned Dr. R. about the whereabouts of the trust general secretary and the man who was treated for poisoning. At about 7:00 P.M., H., the ambulance driver, was taken to another room and made to strip to his underclothes. H. stated that the police told him to tell them where the general secretary and the militant were hiding. He told them that he was only on duty from 9:00 A.M. until 5:00 P.M. and that no such case had come to the hospital during that time. Then he was told to get dressed and was taken to another room. While they were questioning him, the police punched him several times on his ears. His right ear began to bleed, and he lost his hearing for a month. He and Dr. R. were released the next day at 2:00 P.M.

Dr. R. stated that the police had questioned him about the type of poison the man had consumed. Dr. R. told them that he had been on leave at the time and that the man might have been treated by Dr. C.,

III. Human Rights Violations by Government Forces

who was at the time in Patiala. The police raided the place where Dr. C. was staying in Patiala, but found he had left for Simla. Police arrested his father and brother, and brought them to the Saddar police station. They were released the next day on the condition that they produce Dr. C.. When Dr. C. returned on May 17, he and his brother and Dr. R. went to the police station at 6:00 P.M. He was questioned and released at 7:30 P.M.

On May 14, 1992, R. Singh, aged thirty-five, a generator operator at the Sarabha Memorial Hospital, was also detained at the Sudhar police station. He was made to lie on a cot and a white cloth was put over his face. The police tied his ankles with rope and one policeman pulled on his feet while another pulled him by the hair. The police poured water onto the cloth until he felt "as if he was drowning." From time to time, the police stopped and asked him where the man who had taken poison had been taken. After that the police tortured him with the roller. He was detained for ten days but was not beaten again. When Dr. Iacopino examined R. in October 1992, he was found to have circular scars around both ankles, consistent with abrasions from rope burns that could have been caused by being suspended.

T. Singh and R. Singh

R. Singh, aged twenty-eight, a resident of Dakha, told HRW/PHR that at the time of his wedding on January 23, 1991, some militants from the neighborhood, who were with the Khalistan Commando Force (Zaffarwal) came to the ceremony to ensure that the family was not providing any liquor or dowry.[68] After they had satisfied themselves that this was the case, they left.

About one month later, plainclothes police of the Dakha police station detained R.'s younger brother T. Singh, aged twenty-two. During interrogation they asked T. to name the militants who had come to the wedding. T. told him that he did not know the militants' whereabouts. Then the police took T. to a brick kiln where they forced him to strip, and then two of the policemen pulled his legs out to either side. Then he was taken to the Dakha police station, where the police put on their

---

[68] Many of the militants attempted to impose a code of conduct in Punjab, prohibiting the sale and consumption of liquor, dictating dress codes for women and forbidding any practices that were considered "Hindu", like dowry.

uniforms and took T. to CIA staff headquarters in Ludhiana. They kept him there for four days, and he was suspended by his hands and beaten. T. said that whenever he asked for water the police would taunt him, saying, "Oh, you want to drink?" Then they would take a full bath tumbler and pour it into the back of his mouth and nose until he choked. The family was not permitted to see him, but the police did permit a friend of the family, a retired major, to see T. When the major told Inspector Manmohan Singh of the CIA staff that T. was innocent and had no information on the whereabouts of the militants, he was released. He had bruises and rope marks on his legs and difficulty walking. He received medical treatment for two months, and then left the village to take a job with a trucking company.

On March 18, 1992, police from the Sudharat police station again arrested T., along with his brothers R. and B., aged seventeen, and his brothers-in-law, G., aged eighteen, and B., aged seventeen. They were taken to the Sudhar police station; T. and R. were kept separate from the others. They were interrogated about the whereabouts of Jagga Singh, the only one of the militants who had come to the wedding who was still alive at that time. They denied knowing anything. Then R. was taken to SHO Randhir Singh's room where he was stripped naked and his hands were tied behind his back. One policeman put his knee in R.'s back and pulled his hair back while two others pulled his legs out to the side. After being tortured in this way for two days, the police told him that T. had been killed so he might as well tell them what they wanted to know. However, one of the jail staff workers told R. that T. was still alive.

On March 24, a number of prominent men from the village interceded with the police, and R. was released to them at about 3:00 P.M. T. was released on April 3 or 4. He had been tortured in the same way as R. Both men stated that they received medical treatment for their injuries for several months after their release.[69]

When PHR examined R. in October 1992, R. complained of pain in the inner left thigh. The physical examination revealed tenderness of one of the left thigh muscles, especially near the pelvis. The pain was exacerbated by outward movement of the legs.

---

[69] On October 3, 1992, the police again came to arrest R., but when he ran away, they arrested his brother, B.. For more on the case, see p.53.

B. Singh

B. Singh, aged thirty-seven, a travel agent and resident of Ludhiana, was arrested[70] on April 1, 1992, after the Superintendent of Police of Tiwana was killed in a bomb blast about four kilometers outside Ludhiana. At about 11:00 P.M., police from the Sarabha Nagar police station picked B. up from his residence and took him to the CIA staff headquarters. About forty other men were also brought in that night. B. told us that he was beaten with straps and lathis and questioned about the militants. He was tortured by having his legs stretched out to the sides, being suspended from the ceiling by a rope, and by having a heavy wooden roller pressed over his legs. He was also punched in the head and slapped on the ears. He was detained for ten days. He was detained again once in May and five times in June 1992 for a total of ten days. No charges were filed against him.

At the time of B.'s examination by Dr. Iacopino in October 1992, he was found to have tenderness over the lower vertebrae and other symptoms indicative of disk disease with nerve damage, as well as decreased hearing and a purulent discharge from the right ear.

A. Singh

On August 11, 1992, at about 5:30 A.M., police surrounded the houses of M. Singh and his brother, A. Singh, in the village of Latala, in district Ludhiana. The police beat A. Singh and his wife, N. and forced them into a police van. When they passed a bus stand about one hundred yards from the house, A. was taken out and put in a separate van. N. was taken to the Sudhar police station and kept there for four days. She was not beaten again.

A. Singh stated that the police came into his room while he was asleep, grabbed him by the hair, and dragged him into the courtyard. The police were led by SHO Darshan Singh of the Dehlon police station. With him was constable Avtar Singh of the Latala police post and about seven other policemen. They beat him with their rifle butts and fists on his head and abdomen. Then SHO Darshan Singh told the other policemen, "*Chade parho*" ("stretch the legs"). The policemen ordered A. to strip, and

---

[70] B. Singh had been arrested and tortured repeatedly between 1984 and 1992.

then one of them stood behind him with a knee at A.'s back while two others pulled his legs out straight to the sides. At the same time, an officer whom A. described as having three stars on his lapel kicked him in the hips with his boots. Then A. was told to dress and dragged over to the police van. At the bus stand, he was moved to another van in which his cousin, Hardeep Singh, was lying unconscious.[71] A. was released on August 19 without ever being told why he had been detained.

S. Singh

S. Singh, aged forty-two, a resident of Amritsar, told us that he was arrested[72] at around midnight on January 1, 1992, by police from the CIA staff headquarters in Ludhiana, led by Inspector Manmohan Singh.[73] They took him to the Civil Lines police station and interrogated him until 4:00 A.M. The police ordered S. to remove his clothes and sit on the floor. One policeman then pulled him by his hair, while two pulled on his legs and two others pulled his arms. Another man was detained in the same room, and when the police brought S. back they threatened the man that they would torture him as they had done with S. unless he told them the whereabouts of his son.

At about 9:00 A.M. on January 2, four plainclothes policemen, one of whom was referred to as "Pinky"[74], came into the room. S was again ordered to remove his clothes and his hands were tied behind his back with a rope and then hoisted up until he fainted. On January 3, an article

---

[71] For more on what happened to Hardeep Singh, see p.39

[72] S. Singh had previously been arrested during the Indian army's assault on the Golden Temple in June 1984 and held in an army camp for two months. He was tortured there, and then jailed in Amritsar's Central Jail. He was charged with attempting to overthrow the government, but the case against him was dismissed in 1985. He was again arrested in December 1990, and tortured for fifteen days. He was accused of assisting the militants, but no case was registered against him.

[73] Manmohan Singh was subsequently promoted to deputy superintendent in Ludhiana.

[74] "Pinky" was reported to be a "cat" -- an informer.

III. Human Rights Violations by Government Forces 81

about S.'s detention appeared in the Punjabi daily *Ajit*. The next day, at about noon, S. was called into see Manmohan Singh and SSP Raj Kishan Bedi. SSP Bedi said:

> You seem to be a respected gentleman. If you take some money and arms from us you will lead a comfortable life. Get hold for us those terrorists whom you know and we will provide you protection. Why do you want to get your arms and legs unnecessarily broken by us?

When S. refused, Manmohan Singh said to him,

> We are giving you until 4:00 A.M. Think it over. If you do not agree, we will kill you and show you as killed in an "encounter."

S. was then taken back to the lock-up. At 8:00 A.M., "Pinky" told him, "We have been approached to have you released, but we are also giving you time to think it over." S. was left for several days.

On January 10, 1992, at about noon, S. was brought before DIG Shekhar, who asked him a few questions and then sent him back to the lock-up. On January 11, at about 3:00 P.M., SSP Bedi called S. to his room and told him that they had concluded that he was innocent. He told S. that he should let the police know if any militant comes to his house. Then S. was released.

On March 26, 1992, as S. was leaving his office at about 10:00 A.M., two men in civilian clothes grabbed him, blindfolded him and forced him into a car. They told him that they were with a militant group, and that they believed he was an informer. But when the car reached an army checkpoint and stopped, the men identified themselves to the police as police and were allowed to pass. After that, the car stopped again and S. was taken into a room, the blindfold was removed and he saw that he was at a CRPF camp.

An SP then told him that he had been released from police custody on the condition that he inform on the militants, and he had not done so. The SP then told him:

> I have instructions from higher officials to show results. Punjab is having a fever; if we kill fifteen or sixteen

militants it is like an ice pack bringing down the temperature and they are satisfied.

Then the SP told S. he would release him, but that S. should provide the police with information. S. was then released.

When PHR examined S. in October 1992, he had some pain and decreased mobility in his left upper arm.

K. Kaur

K. Kaur, aged twenty-eight, told HRW/PHR that in 1985 her husband, who had been a police constable, deserted to join the Babbar Khalsa militant organization. He was reportedly killed in fighting in 1988. Since then, K. had lived with her mother, R. Kaur, aged forty-five, two sons, aged eight and ten, and a daughter, aged six, in Ludhiana. They had not had problems with the police during this time.

On March 28, 1992, about sixteen police from the Sector 39 police station in Chandigarh, came to the house and questioned K. about a man whom they claimed had escaped from the hospital while in judicial custody. K. stated:

> They took me and my parents to the Sector 39 police station, and then to the Sector 11 police station on the same day. They asked me questions about this boy, but I didn't know anything about him. I was slapped and thrown to the ground. Several men stretched my legs apart. The pain was unbearable. Then, they used two wires with clips to give electric shocks to my ears and toes. I lost consciousness twice. While I was still sitting on the floor, they moved a heavy roller over my thighs. After five days, I was released. My thighs were badly bruised and swollen.

K.'s mother, R., told PHR/HRW that while she was detained at the Sector 11 police station, she could hear her daughter's screams.

K. was arrested again on June 4, 1992, along with some neighbors. The arrests were witnessed by members of the village panchayat. The police accused her of sheltering militants. When she denied it, she was tortured with electric shocks, leg stretching and the

III. Human Rights Violations by Government Forces

roller. She stated that she was also suspended upside-down by her ankles until she lost consciousness. She was released the following day after the family paid a Rs.50,000 [$1,670] bribe to the police and the panchayat assured the police that she would not harbor militants or leave the village.

When PHR examined K. in October 1992, she had muscle damage of the right thigh, consistent with injuries caused by the roller method of torture. She also had scars, indicative of abrasions and lacerations on the right foot and both shin areas.

B. Singh

J. Singh, aged fifty-six, a draftsman from Chandigarh, told PHR/HRW that on January 1, 1991, at about 7:00 P.M., ten to twelve police, including SHO Satnam Randhawa Singh and SI Anokh Singh, came to his house. The police demanded to see J.'s son, B., aged twenty-two, a student who had had no prior problems with the police. The police searched J.'s house for several hours but nothing was found. The police then picked up B. from a relative's house in Mohali and took him to the Sector 17 police station in Chandigarh. B.'s family initially was able to visit him in the police station. On January 11, the local newspapers published a police report in which it was alleged that B. and several others were involved in an exchange of gunfire with police in Chandigarh.

B. was produced in court on January 11, 1991, before magistrate Jagjit Puri and remanded to police custody for fourteen days. During the two-week remand, J. was not permitted contact with his son. On January 24, B. was transferred to Model Jail in Chandigarh. When J. visited his son at the jail, B. told him that he had been tortured for five days at the Sector 17 Police Station. J. said that B. walked with difficulty and had bruises on his arms and legs. B. was released on bail May 1, 1991.

On or about July 6, 1991, at 11:00 P.M., some twenty police from CIA staff in Sector 11, including Inspector Satvir Singh and SI Gurnam Singh, came to J. home looking for B. Finding that B. was not there, the police detained another one of J.'s sons, I., aged thirty-two, an engineer. I. told us what happened to him at the police station:

> They asked me questions about my brother, B., about his activities and where he was staying. They slapped me,

pulled my hair out and insulted the women in my family. After three hours, they released me after someone brought a message to the police with an address for B.

Several days later the police returned to J.'s home and threatened to "pick up the entire family." As a result, the entire family left the house that day. J. contacted SSP Saini and pleaded for police not to arrest B. The SSP demanded that B. be brought to him. On the following day, B. went to the SSP and after the SSP entered his name in a book, he was taken into custody at CIA Staff, Sector 11. On August 8, SSP Saini called the parents into the police station. In the presence of his parents, B. was slapped and insulted. SSP Saini told them, "He hasn't admitted anything. We need arms from him." He told them that B. would be released on August 15, but he was not. Jagjit immediately sent letters about B.'s case to the Chief Justice and the Prime Minister.

On September 17, B. was produced in court and charged with "harboring terrorists." He was sent to Model Jail and released on bail on October 23. In January 1992, the family's home was again raided. B.'s family subsequently canceled his bail on February 6 so that B. could remain in jail for his own protection. After that, J. approached SSP Saini who assured him that B. would not be picked up arbitrarily. B. was then released on bail on March 27. However, he was picked up immediately and taken first to Sector 19 police station, and then to the Sector 26 police station. His family was able to see him on a daily basis. He told them that he was not tortured at that time.

On April 11, 1992, B. was brought to court and charged with "possession of weapons." The First Information Report (FIR)[75] was dated April 11 rather than March 27, when he was actually arrested. He was remanded to police custody for three days, and then sent to Model Jail. Believing that B. was safer in jail than outside, the family decided not to press for bail.

K. Singh

K. Singh was arrested on July 31, 1991 along with two friends of his, Swaran Singh and Daljit Singh. All three men were separately taken

---

[75] A First Information Report is filed by police. It is the starting point for any police investigation into a crime.

III. Human Rights Violations by Government Forces

into a room, stripped, suspended by a rope from the ceiling and beaten with leather straps and lathis.

On August 1, at 4:00 A.M., K. was taken out of the lock-up. The police again tied a rope around his ankles. He described what happened next:

> They hung me upside down and poured water in my nose and mouth until I thought I was going to suffocate. They also beat me with a leather strap which had the words "Meet me my friend" painted on with white paint. Sometimes they lowered me and then brought me up again. They beat me with an iron rod on ankles and arms. Some of the police were drunk. After they took me back to the lock-up, I saw Daljit being taken out at about 10:00 A.M., and Swaran after him. I could hear their cries. They were brought back about an hour later. They could not walk and were being carried by the police. On August 2 at about 4:00 A.M. I saw them being taken out again.

Daljit and Swaran were reportedly killed on August 3. On August 5, K. was produced in court and charged with murder and harboring terrorists.[76] K. was sent to judicial custody in the central jail in Amritsar and released on bail after two months on medical grounds. He had seen the prison doctor for the numbness in arms and legs and an infected wound on his hand he had sustained when he was beaten with the iron rod, but was not admitted to the prison hospital because they told him they did not have the medicine to treat him. When he petitioned the prison medical board and told them he had been tortured, the board recommended that he be granted bail on grounds that he was not being provided medical care. The medical board's report was filed in court. After being released on bail, K. was detained four or five times. In September 1992 he was detained by DSP Mohinder Singh for two days but not charged.

When PHR's Dr. Iacopino examined K. in October 1992, K. had a four-centimeter fluid filled cyst over the right shin bone. A callus under

---

[76] First Information Report dated July 25, 1991. K. was charged under Sections 302 and 216 of the Indian Penal Code.

the cyst suggested an old fracture. He also had a four-centimeter scar over the right shoulder and pain in the left shoulder.

Ba. Singh

Ba. Singh, aged twenty-one, a resident of Baina Bulund Village, told us about his arrest and torture in August 1991.[77]

> On the day before Rakhe [a holiday which usually falls in March or April], at about 4:00 A.M., police surrounded our house, and then jumped the wall to our family compound and arrested me. They did not tell my family where they were taking me. When we got into the police van they began beating me with their fists. They asked me where my brother was. I told them that I did not know. We were taken to the CIA staff headquarters in Patiala and placed in a room. After about fifteen minutes, I was taken to the courtyard. They forced me to remove my clothes. When I refused to remove my underwear, I was beaten with lathis and someone removed them. Four or five policemen began beating me with lathis. My hands were tied behind my back and I was suspended from a rope that was hanging from a tree branch. While I was suspended in the air they beat the soles of my feet with lathis until I lost consciousness. I regained consciousness when they threw water on my face. They asked more questions about my brother, then told me to "get up and run." Each time I stopped or slowed down, they beat my ankles with lathis. At daybreak, I was brought back to the cell.

---

[77] Before August 1991, Ba. had been detained at the CIA staff headquarters in Patiala and the Sadar police station several times when the police were looking for his brother. The duration of these detentions ranged from five to ten days. The police beat him on the soles of his feet with wooden rods. They also beat him on the back with leather belts, one of which had the words "Meet me my friend" written on one side and "We will meet again" on the other. Other detainees have also described being beaten with these belts. See, for example, the case of K. Singh, the discussion of which begins on p.84.

III. Human Rights Violations by Government Forces

At about noon the following day, Ba. was taken to the courtyard and forced to disrobe. His legs were repeatedly forced apart, then he was made to "get up and run" as before. After this, he was tortured with the roller.

> My hands were still tied behind my back and I was sitting on the ground. Someone held my hair and forced his knee in my back. Three policemen stood on a heavy wooden roller as two others moved the roller over my thighs. I screamed in pain and after a few minutes lost consciousness. Water was thrown on my face to wake me. I asked for a drink of water, but was given just a few sips. When I asked for more, they threw hot water in my face. Again, they stretched my legs and used the roller until I lost consciousness. Eventually, a boy dressed me and two policemen carried me to my cell.

Ba. stated that Inspector Grewal had given the policemen orders to torture him and was present during the torture.

On the following day, Ba. was again tortured with leg stretching and the roller. By this time, he had difficulty standing. For the next two days he was periodically forced to "run" in the courtyard. When he could not, the police beat his legs with lathis. Then he was left alone for about five days. During the five days after that, he was again tortured with leg stretching, suspension, the roller and electric shocks to his ears and penis. He lost consciousness many times. Then five days passed without further torture. After a total of three to four weeks he was released. He was never brought before the court nor were charges filed against him.

Approximately three months later, police from Patiala arrested Ba. at the *gurdwara* (Sikh temple) where he worked. He was taken to the Sadar police station in Ambala. There, he was subjected to severe beatings, forced leg stretching, the roller and electric shocks to his penis. He was released after eight days. No charges were filed and he was not produced in court. Because the police continued to visit the gurdwara, Ba. quit his job there.

When Ba. was examined by Dr. Iacopino in October 1992, he had signs of an old fracture of the right second front rib, three skull deformities, a small scar on the left ear consistent a burn from electric shock and several small scars on the penis.

S. Kaur and son A. Singh

S. Kaur, aged fifty-one, a teacher from Mohali, told HRW/PHR in October 1992 that on May 29, 1991, she and her son, A. Swaran, aged nineteen, were arrested by police, accused of providing shelter to militants and taken to the Sector 39 police station in Chandigarh. She stated:

> When we arrived at the police station, they separated me from my son. I was taken to a room in which there were about five policemen and SSP Saini. He asked me questions about some militants who he claimed had visited our home. When I told him that we knew nothing about any militants, the policemen began slapping and punching me in the face. They threatened to take off my clothes and to kill my son. Then one of them pulled me by the hair and threw me to the ground. They forced me to lie on my stomach and stood on my hands. They rolled a heavy wooden roller repeatedly over the backs of my legs. They also stretched my legs apart many times and used electric shocks to my body. After several hours of this, they brought my son into the room. They held him by his hair and kicked him. Then, he was forced to sit on the floor and they stretched his legs apart about five or six times. He lost consciousness and fell, hitting his head on the ground. His head was bleeding. After this, I was taken to a cell in which there were three other women and five or six men. I was released two days later and my son was released three days after me.

Since being tortured, S. Kaur has experienced chronic pain in her thigh and calf muscles, especially in cold weather. The physical examination conducted by the PHR demonstrated signs of muscle damage in her legs, consistent with damage that would have been caused by the roller treatment.

S. Kaur told us that A. Singh was again picked up by the police on September 5, 1992, and detained at the Mohali Police Station for three days, where he was again tortured.

G. Singh and Others

G., aged thirty, a resident of Baina Bulund village, was detained by the police in March 1991.[78] He, together with his two brothers, M., aged thirty-five, and S., aged forty, were taken to the CIA staff headquarters in Patiala. There, G. was taken into a room, stripped naked and his hands were tied behind his back. The police interrogated him about a relative who had joined a militant group, and when he denied knowing the relative's whereabouts, the police began beating him. He was also given electric shock to the ears by means of wires attached to a hand-cranked generator. One of the policemen administering the shocks was Inspector Sant Kumar. The torture continued for about twenty minutes. G. was then taken back to the room, and his two brothers were each taken out and given the same treatment. On the evening of that day, G. was taken to the same room and beaten by some ten to fifteen policemen. One of them took out a revolver and threatened to shoot G. unless he told them the whereabouts of his relative.

G.'s brother S. described a similar treatment:

> When I was taken into the room, there were six policemen there, including Inspector Sant Kumar, who slapped me and punched me, asking, "Why do you give shelter to [a militant] and why do you not tell us where he is?" He told me they would shoot my brother unless I told. Then they took me back to the room. When they brought G. back, two policemen were holding him up. He was in bad shape and nearly unconscious. For four days, he could not drink water on his own and we could only pour small amounts in his mouth.

G.'s brothers were released after eight days. The day after they were released, G. was again taken out of the room. The police tied his hair

---

[78] The family had been harassed by the police repeatedly. Family members have been assaulted, detained and tortured by police as a means of pressuring them to reveal information about a relative who was wanted by the police. After the relative was reportedly killed in an "encounter" in June 1992, the police visits became less frequent but did not stop.

with a rope and tied his hands behind his back and then beat him. He was released after sixteen days. He was never produced before a magistrate or court, and no case was ever registered against him.

After M. L. Manchanda, an engineer with All-India Radio in Chandigarh, was shot and then beheaded by militants on May 18, 1992, the police from the Sadar Patiala police station came to G.'s house looking for him every day for four days, and finally arrested him from the home of his aunt in Barnala. He was again taken to the CIA staff headquarters in Patiala. His aunt was detained with him, along with her infant. After three or four days, she was released with the child. G. was released after eight days.

IV. VIOLATIONS OF HUMANITARIAN LAW BY MILITANTS

All of the known militant organizations operating in Punjab have committed flagrant violations of international human rights and humanitarian law. Human Rights Watch/Asia and PHR believe that, at least up until mid-1992, the extent of conflict in Punjab rose to the level of application of international humanitarian law, particularly Common Article 3 to the Geneva Conventions, which protects non-combatants in armed conflicts.[79] The militant groups which operated in Punjab between 1980 and 1993 flagrantly and routinely violated the provisions of international humanitarian law. Among the most egregious of these abuses have been targeted attacks on Hindu and Sikh civilians, calculated to sow terror among the local population and to compel members of the Hindu minority community to leave Punjab.[80] In twelve years of conflict there were many examples of such attacks, some of which occurred outside Punjab in neighboring states or in Delhi. Militant groups massacred bus and train passengers, detonated bombs in markets, restaurants and residential areas, and gunned down residents of Hindu neighborhoods.

In 1992, many of the militant groups began deliberately targeting the families of police. In the course of the year at least 133 people, many of them children, were killed in these attacks. We investigated one of these cases, which is discussed below. The attacks on police relatives subsided after mid-1992, following the killings of most of the militant leaders.

Militant groups also assassinated civil servants, politicians, journalists, businessmen, and other prominent individuals, including moderate Sikh political leaders who opposed the militants. Candidates for

---

[79] For more on the provisions of Common Article 3, see footnote 20.

[80] As a result, thousands of Hindus have fled the state over the last seven years. Hindu migrant laborers, known as *purbeas*["easterners"] from eastern states of India, particularly Bihar, have been the victims of some of these killings. These migrants have traditionally provided labor for Sikh farmers. The motive for their killing appears to be both an attempt to terrorize the minority population and to drive out competing labor. See Susanne Rudolph, "Why India's Militant Sikhs Keep Fighting," *Christian Science Monitor*, March 8, 1989.

election to the parliament and state assembly were particularly targeted during the elections of 1991 and 1992. Militant groups have also killed suspected collaborators or informers. In late 1990 and early 1991, militant groups issued "codes of conduct" for journalists, requiring that they broadcast programs in Punjabi, adopt the militants' terminology and publish press statements released by the militant groups.

Militants also kidnapped civilians for the purposes of extortion or to secure the release of detained colleagues, and have frequently murdered their victims. When militant organizations have claimed responsibility for particular acts of violence, they have generally done so through local newspapers. However many acts of violence go unclaimed, and it is impossible to say which, if any, of the various groups is responsible.

We were not in a position to investigate many of the hundreds of such attacks which have taken place. Most of those described below occurred in 1990 or 1991, and they represent only a small portion of the abuses for which militant groups are believed responsible. Since 1992, militant attacks have sharply decreased but have not stopped altogether. Below, we describe several incidents which occurred in 1993. In all of the incidents documented, militants killed, wounded or threatened civilians. Such acts directly contravene international law, which prohibits acts of violence against civilians.

Not all of the militant groups professed the same ideological or political goals, and over the years of conflict they have frequently been at odds with one another.[81] They were organized into at least seven major groups -- all theoretically operate under the authority of one of a number of Panthic Committees which functioned as decision-making

---

[81] Most of the militant groups in Punjab trace their origins to Sant Bhindranwale, a charismatic Sikh preacher who rose to prominence in the mid-1970s and gained a reputation early on as a fiery orator and rigid fundamentalist. By 1978, he had gained the backing of Congress (I) political leaders who saw in him an opportunity to discredit the Akali Dal - Janata Dal coalition government then in power in Punjab. As Bhindranwale became more powerful, the Akali Dal also attempted to court Bhindranwale in order to attract his following. Rival Akali factions fell out over this policy and supported other militant factions. Bhindranwale was killed when the Indian army stormed the Golden Temple in 1984. Since his death, the number of groups proliferated -- as did the divisions among them.

IV. Violations of Humanitarian Law by Militants

bodies and issue instructions. The Panthic Committee headed by Dr. Sohan Singh was historically the most powerful and is supported by the Khalistan Commando Force (Panjwar), Babbar Khalsa, Khalistan Liberation Force (Budhisingwala), Bhindranwale Tiger Force of Khalistan (Sangha) and the Sikh Students Federation (Bittu). Sohan Singh was captured in November 1993. The Panthic Committee headed by Gurbachan Singh Manochahal was supported by the Bhindranwale Tiger Force (Manochahal) and the Khalistan Commando Force (Rajasthani group). The Zaffarwal Panthic Committee was supported by the Khalistan Commando Force (Zaffarwal).[82] However, at least some of these groups operated independently of the committee with some operating as loosely-organized armed gangs.

Indian authorities have long claimed that Sikh militants receive arms and training from Pakistan. It is unlikely that official Pakistani support for Sikh militants ever reached the level of assistance provided to Kashmiri militants, but, given the porous nature of Punjab's border and the availability of sophisticated weaponry, it was relatively easy for the militants to find safe haven and a ready supply of arms in Pakistan. As one long-time observer of Indian politics has noted, over the years of the conflict,

> Arms were regularly smuggled across the border, and it is more than likely that President Zia [of Pakistan] turned a blinder eye than usual. It is certain that he did not object to Bhindranwale's terrorists crossing the border to seek temporary refuge from the police.

He notes, however, that, "Zia adopted a very cautious attitude to the Punjab crisis,"[83] an opinion shared by another journalist who adds that "the level of assistance to the guerrillas from Pakistan's government appears to be lower than in Kashmir...some guerrillas say that they conduct their own training and only cross into Pakistan to purchase

---

[82] See Monimoy Dasgupta, "Militants are Getting Tired of Fighting: Taksal," *Telegraph*, February 17, 1991; and ibid, "Doctor May Plan Militants' Strategy," *Telegraph*, April 25, 1991

[83] Tully and Jacob, p.212.

weapons."[84] In fact, security forces on both sides reportedly have had a hand in the arms smuggling.[85]

Executions of Civilians

At the time of our mission in October 1992, killings of civilians by militant groups had declined substantially, largely because the police had already killed many of the militant leaders and the remaining militants were attempting to avoid capture. The exception to this pattern was the large-scale killings of family members of police, which escalated dramatically in early 1992. Many of the killings followed the killings of militant leaders. For example, militants killed some forty-two relatives of policemen in August 1992 alone after Sukhdev Singh Babbar, head of the Babbar Khalsa, and Gujrant Singh Budhsinghwala, the head of the Khalistan Liberation Force, were killed by police. We investigated one of these incidents which took place in the village of Boparai.

Massacre in Boparai

According to B. Singh, on August 10, 1992, at about 9:15 A.M., five gunmen came to the house and ordered the family outside. They asked if the eldest son, S. Singh, was a constable with the Punjab police. When told that he was, the gunmen told M. Singh, his brother Mh. Singh, aged sixty-two, his wife J. Singh, aged forty-five, their son D. Singh, aged sixteen, daughter G. Kaur, aged twelve, and son S. Singh, aged seven, to sit against the courtyard wall. Then they opened fire. When the daughter, G., ducked through a doorway to hide in an adjacent building, several of the militants followed her inside and shot her there. They then told the remaining relatives that the killings had been done because one member of the family was with the police, and warned them that if they told anyone about the incident, they would also be killed. The family believed they were with the Khalistan Liberation Front, as a young man from the neighborhood had joined that group and knew their family. After the

---

[84] Steve Coll, "India, Pakistan Wage Covert Proxy Wars,'" *Washington Post*, December 8, 1990.

[85] James Clad, "Terrorism's Toll," *Far Eastern Economic Review*, October 11, 1990, p. 34.

IV. Violations of Humanitarian Law by Militants

incident, the family no longer stayed in the house at night. They told us, "We are living in constant fear."

Other Attacks on Civilians

- Civilians who have defied militant orders have also been the victims of murder and assault. We investigated an incident which took place on October 9, 1992, at about 8:00 P.M., in which G.R., aged thirty-six, a shopkeeper and an active member of the Congress party, and his son K. were shot. The men were returning home when they saw two men brandishing pistols standing on a street corner. G. told HRW that he heard one of the men call him by name. The men then told G. and K. to run, and then opened fire. G. was shot in the chest and right arm. K. was shot in the right shoulder. G. had kept his shop opened during a strike called by the militants some weeks earlier, and believed that the attack may have been in retaliation for that incident.

Killings of civilians by militant groups peaked in 1990 and 1991.[86] Deliberate attacks on Hindus or non-Punjabis escalated in these years as on several occasions, militants also stopped buses and other vehicles and, after identifying Hindu passengers, murdered them. According to official figures, some fifteen hundred Hindu families sought refuge in relief camps in Delhi between 1986 and 1992. In June 1991, militants opened fire on two passenger trains in Punjab, killing at least one hundred and ten civilians. Such incidents continued in 1992, particularly after the election of a Congress-I state government under Chief Minister Beant Singh in February.

During the campaigns for the national and state assembly elections in May and June 1991, twenty-four candidates in Punjab were assassinated. In some cases, those assassinated were members of political parties long perceived as opponents on the militants. The principal victims were politicians and political candidates, primarily from the

---

[86] According to press reports, in 1988 an estimated 2,500 persons were killed by all forces, militants and police, and in 1989, the total was 3,000. Estimates of the total number of persons killed in 1990 range as high as 4,500. In the first half of 1991 an estimated 2,000 civilians were killed. How many of these represent civilians is impossible to say, particularly since a large percentage of those listed officially as "terrorists" killed by the security forces are also civilians.

Congress-I, Communist Party of India (CPI) and Bharatiya Janata Party (BJP) parties. Because a number of militant factions fielded candidates, some say the assassinations may have been due to conflicts among these groups.[87] Attacks on political figures continued after the polls.

- On September 24, 1993, three Congress-I party workers were killed when unidentified gunmen opened fire on their car outside the town of Ludhiana. The men were on their way to attend a Congress-I rally scheduled for the next day.[88]

- On February 23, 1993, at least five people were killed and thirty-five injured when bombs exploded in the city of Jammu, the winter capital of the north Indian state of Jammu and Kashmir. The two bombs, which police said had been planted in a motorcycle and probably activated by a timer, exploded in the busy Indira Chowk area of the city. A Sikh militant group called Khalistan Zindabad (Long Live Khalistan) claimed responsibility, saying it was revenge for what the group described as communal killings in 1989.[89]

- On June 23, 1992, two militants on a motor-scooter shot the Amritsar Congress-I president, Multan Singh, and his bodyguard, Lakhwinder Singh, as they stepped out of Multan Singh's house in the Mikka Singh Colony of Amritsar. Multan Singh died from his injuries on

---

[87] The elections were originally scheduled for May 20-26, 1991, but following the May 21 assassination of Congress-I candidate Rajiv Gandhi at an election rally in Tamil Nadu, completion of the polling in all states but Assam and Punjab was postponed until June 12 and 15. The Assam polls took place on June 6. The Punjab polls were scheduled to be held on June 22. No election was held in Jammu and Kashmir.

[88] "Three Congress-I Workers Killed by Punjab Rebels," All India Radio, September 24, 1993, as cited in Foreign Broadcast Information Service (FBIS-NES-93-185), September 27, 1993, p. 62.

[89] Reuters, "Indian Bomb Blast Kills Five, Sparks Rioting," February 23, 1994 and Sikh Militants Claim Kashmir Blast," February 24, 1994.

IV. Violations of Humanitarian Law by Militants

the way to the hospital. Lakhwinder, who was seriously injured, had been on the militants' hit list.[90]

- On March 10, 1992, gunmen entered a factory near Sangrur and, after separating the non-Punjabis from the other workers, shot dead fifteen non-Punjabis.

- On March 14, 1992, militants gunned down eighteen shopkeepers and other civilians in a shopping district in Ludhiana.

Journalists were also targets; several were murdered between 1990 and 1992 following the promulgation of a militant "code of conduct" which prohibited the use of languages other than Punjabi and required that all journalists adopt militant terminology and that newspapers publish the militant groups' statements.

- On May 18, 1992, for example, M.L. Manchanda, an engineer with All-India radio, was kidnapped by militants who demanded that the radio station broadcast only in Punjabi and drop all programming from Delhi. When the station did not comply, the kidnappers shot Manchanda. They then beheaded him, leaving his body to be found in Punjab and his head in the neighboring state of Haryana.

Kidnappings

Militant groups have frequently kidnapped civilians for ransom or to obtain the release of detained members of their organizations. The kidnapping of civilians for money or for the purpose of obtaining the release of detained colleagues is outlawed by Common Article 3, which prohibits "violence to life and person" and the "taking of hostages" with respect to persons taking no part in the hostilities.

Abduction and Murder of Jasbir Singh

Human Rights Watch/Asia and PHR investigated the abduction and murder of Jasbir Singh. On November 2 1991, Jasbir Singh, aged thirty-three, a director at a manufacturing plant in Amritsar, aged thirty-

---

[90]*Tribune* (Chandigarh), June 23, 1992.

three, was stopped in his car by three gunmen. They got in the car and told him to drive on for about five kilometers. They one of the men telephoned Jasbir's uncle, claimed he was a commander with the Khalistan Liberation Front and demanded Rs. 10 million [$330,000] in ransom. Jasbir's uncle told the man that he needed time to think it over and then notified the police. The police put a tap on the family's phone and they identified the place where Jasbir was being held as Varpal, about six kilometers outside Amritsar. However, when the army and police tried to surround the area, the militants escaped. Jasbir was then killed. The family continued to receive telephoned threats after the incident by callers who said that they would abduct another family member. The family said that the calls stopped after the killings of many top militants in mid-1992.

V. CONCLUSION AND RECOMMENDATIONS

Indian officials who are eager to reassure their critics that the country's democratic institutions do more than enough to protect human rights point to the "success" of the February 1992 elections in Punjab and the restoration of a civilian state administration there after years of direct rule from New Delhi. But the 1992 elections did not mean the restoration of the rule of law in the state. On the contrary, the police, while nominally answerable to the new government under Chief Minister Beant Singh, have remained a force that is accountable to no one but Director-General of Police K.P.S. Gill. There are credible allegations that Gill himself authorized and condoned human rights violations. Subsequent local elections held at the district and municipal levels in 1992 and 1993 followed on the heels of police operations in which countless civilians were tortured, "disappeared" and murdered.

While few in the Indian government will admit so publicly, many privately acknowledge that in DGP Gill's zeal to end the violence, he has created a police force whose tactics and abuses are the very same as those of the militants. Diplomats and journalists in India report that the Punjab police have lost their ability to conduct investigations, that they routinely resort to extortion and other abuses, and that they consider a reputation for being a torturer as a means to getting a swift promotion.

Most disturbing is the fact that many in India's central government see the "Punjab solution" as an appropriate policy to implement in other areas of conflict, notably Kashmir. Although recent moves to appoint Gill to Kashmir were scuttled by the state's governor, it is clear that his methods -- torture, disappearances and murder -- have not only been sanctioned, but are actively promoted at senior levels of government as a justifiable means to an end. It is a legacy that will haunt India for decades to come.

In late 1993, India established a national human rights commission empowered to investigate reports of abuse and to recommend prosecution or other punitive measures. We believe that the incidents of abuse documented in this report represent a test case for the commission's impartiality and independence. The commission should conduct a thorough investigation into the cases documented in this report and call for the criminal prosecution and punishment of police responsible for murder, torture and other egregious abuses. Among those who should be investigated is DGP K.P.S. Gill.

Human Rights Watch/Asia and Physicians for Human Rights also make the following recommendations to the government of India and to the militant organizations operating in Punjab.

- The government of India should support swift investigations of extrajudicial executions, deaths in custody, torture and disappearances by security forces in Punjab. Security personnel responsible for these abuses should be prosecuted in civilian courts. Only with such trials and appropriate punishments will these forces receive the clear, unequivocal message that human rights violations are not condoned by their superiors. Those found guilty of abuse should be punished regardless of rank. Members of the police or military should not be treated more leniently than other persons found guilty of committing serious crimes, such as murder and torture; indeed, because of their role as members of the military or police, theirs are aggravated forms of these crimes. The results of these investigations and the punishments should be made public as a means of giving the people of Punjab a reason to believe in the government's commitment to justice and the rule of law. Victims or their family members should be paid compensation.

- Physicians in Punjab should be permitted to carry out post mortems in all cases of unnatural death. If necessary, training should be provided to physicians to insure the consistency and thoroughness of the post mortem. It may also be necessary to provide community

V. Conclusion and Recommendations

education to answer religious and cultural concerns about the process. Those conducting post mortems must be able to function impartially and independently of any potentially implicated persons or organizations.

- Detainees should have access to prompt medical examinations by civil medical staff. The results of those examinations and all post mortem reports should be automatically available to the courts and to the detainee's family and legal counsel.

- The government of India should strengthen and enforce the safeguards existing in Indian law that protect detainees from torture, including requirements that all arrests be made pursuant to warrants, that all detainees be brought before a magistrate or other judicial authority empowered to review the legality of the arrest within twenty-four hours of arrest, and that all detainees have immediate and regular access to lawyers, family members and medical care. A centralized register of detainees accessible to lawyers and family members should be established in the state. In addition, the security agencies should require that arresting officers provide signed receipts for all detainees to family members, village elders or persons of similar status. The receipt would be retrieved when the person is released. Security personnel responsible for torture should be held criminally liable and the victims should be compensated.

- The government of India should instruct its security forces in non-lethal methods of crowd control, and amend existing legislation, including the Punjab Disturbed Areas Act and the Punjab Special Powers Act, to curtail the powers granted the security forces to shoot to kill. Provisions immunizing the security forces from prosecution for abuses should be eliminated.

- The government of India should amend the Terrorist and Disruptive Activities Act (TADA) to ensure that provisions overriding the presumption of innocence guaranteed under international law be eliminated, and that confessions made to police officials not in the presence of a magistrate be considered inadmissible as evidence. The government of India should also amend the National Security Act and the TADA to ensure that these laws may not be used to curb legitimate political dissent and free speech.

- The International Committee of the Red Cross should be permitted to undertake the full range of its protection activities in areas of civil conflict in Punjab, and we urge the government of India and all of the militant groups operating in Punjab to extend their full cooperation to the ICRC.

- Militant organizations operating in Punjab should abide by the provisions of international humanitarian law which prohibit killings or other attacks on persons taking no part in the hostilities. Human Rights Watch/Asia and PHR

V. Conclusion and Recommendations

condemn acts of violence by these groups against members of the civilian population.

- Programs should be established in Punjab or in an area accessible to Punjabis to treat victims of physical and psychological trauma resulting from the conflict, including torture. International organizations specializing in such treatment should be permitted access to these programs.